Fantasy Architecture
1500–2036

Neil Bingham
Clare Carolin
Peter Cook
Rob Wilson

D1614372

Hayward Gallery in association with the Royal Institute of British Architects

RIBA 卌

M45793

National Touring Exhibitions
Hayward Gallery

Published on the occasion of *Fantasy Architecture: 1500 – 2036*, a National Touring Exhibition organised by the Hayward Gallery, London for Arts Council England

Exhibition tour:

30 April – 3 July 2004	*Northern Gallery for Contemporary Art, Sunderland*
17 July – 19 September	*The Lowry, Salford*
1 October – 21 November	*New Art Gallery, Walsall*
29 January 2005 – 9 April	*Harris Museum and Art Gallery, Preston*

Exhibition curated by Neil Bingham, Clare Carolin and Rob Wilson
Exhibition organised by Clare Carolin and Rob Wilson
assisted by Rachel Kent

Thanks to bfi Distribution for devising a programme of films to run
in conjunction with *Fantasy Architecture*.

Catalogue designed by SEA
Art Publisher: Caroline Wetherilt
Publishing Co-ordinator: James Dalrymple
Sales Manager: Deborah Power
Printed in The Netherlands by Lecturis

Published by Hayward Gallery Publishing, London SE1 8XX, UK
in association with the Royal Institute of British Architects, London W1B 1AD, UK
© Hayward Gallery 2004
Texts © the authors 2004
Artworks © the artists/architects/architectural firms 2004, unless otherwise stated

Cover montage by SEA/cat.4 (Image by Virtual Artworks), 30, 46, 47, 70, 85, 99, 108, 125
Pages 10-11: William Cameron Menzies, *Things to Come*, 1936 (still) (cat. 87)

The publisher has made every effort to contact all copyright holders. If proper
acknowledgement has not been made, we ask copyright holders to contact the publisher.

ISBN 1 85332 240 7

Hayward Gallery Publishing titles are distributed outside North and South America by Cornerhouse
Publications, 70 Oxford Street, Manchester M1 5NH (tel. +44 (0) 161 200 1503; fax. +44 (0) 161 200 1504;
email: publications@cornerhouse.org; www.cornerhouse.org/publications).

Contents

Preface

Exhibitions made in collaboration with partner organisations are an important element of the Hayward Gallery's National Touring Exhibitions programme and result in some of our most dynamic and stimulating projects. *Fantasy Architecture* began as a conversation with the RIBA Gallery about contemporary art and architecture's current fascination with radical utopian architectural schemes, particularly those of the 1960s. This conversation grew into a project that expanded in many directions, unfolding backwards in time to address the historical precedents of these schemes through the extraordinary material held in the RIBA and V&A collections, and also moving forwards to encompass the realm of computer-aided design, now an integral part of any architectural process.

The wealth of material included in *Fantasy Architecture* shows us how the world might have looked today had the realities of history been different. At the same time it conveys a sense of how close the architecture of the future might bring us to a world already familiar from science fiction films and the fantastic virtual environments of computer games. By juxtaposing a vast range of material in diverse media – from pen and ink sketches to watercolours and computer animations – this exhibition displays the variety of means by which designers use, and have used, images of architecture to capture the imagination of clients and the public.

We are delighted to have had the opportunity to work so closely with the RIBA Gallery and Drawings Collection, and would like to thank Charles Hind, Assistant Director, for his support of the project, which has involved lending a substantial and valuable body of work from the RIBA and V&A Drawings Collections for the duration of the exhibition tour. We also thank Sally Kennedy, Assistant Curator Drawings Collection, Lisa Nash, Conservator, and Liz Towner, Curatorial Assistant, at the RIBA for their help with the very considerable task of preparing the works from the RIBA and V&A collections for display. Thanks also go to Emilie Harrak, Gallery Administrator, and Gina Ha-Gorlin, Exhibition Assistant, for their great help with the sourcing and administration of contemporary works for the exhibition. I am particularly grateful to Rob Wilson, Curator RIBA Gallery, Clare Carolin, Hayward Curator, and Rachel Kent, Hayward Assistant Exhibition Organiser, for co-ordinating the project and bringing it to fruition.

Our discussions around the theme of fantasy architecture began with Neil Bingham, until recently Assistant Curator at the RIBA Drawings Collection, and Rob Wilson, who together with Clare Carolin have curated this exhibition and written this catalogue. We thank Neil and Rob for their illuminating essays on the subject as well as Peter Cook for his lively personal account of the theme.

This catalogue has been edited and produced by the Hayward Gallery, and I extend particular thanks to Caroline Wetherilt, the Hayward's Art Publisher, and James Dalrymple, our Publishing Co-ordinator, for their expertise and attention to it. My thanks also go to Ryan Jones and Bryan Edmondson at SEA for the energy and commitment they have devoted to its design.

I am grateful as well to Helen Luckett, the Hayward's Education Programmer, who has developed an education programme to accompany *Fantasy Architecture*. Thanks go too to d-squared for the innovative resource base that they have designed to accompany the exhibition tour and to B+H Liquid Crystal Resources Ltd for their support in supplying thermochromic materials for the base.

We are delighted that *Fantasy Architecture* will open at Northern Gallery for Contemporary Art where Alistair Robinson is Programme Director. Alistair has been a wholehearted supporter of the project, and an invaluable contributor to its development. We also extend our thanks to the staff of the other venues participating in the exhibition tour for embracing the project with such enthusiasm: Emma Anderson, Curator, and

Sarah Wilcox-Standing, Exhibitions Administrator, at The Lowry, Salford; Deborah Robinson, Acting Director, at The New Art Gallery Walsall; and James Green, Senior Exhibitions Officer, at Harris Museum and Art Gallery, Preston.

This exhibition has benefited from conversations with individuals too numerous to name here but most especially with the architects, artists, designers and lenders to the exhibition who have kindly agreed to part with their work for an extended period. Their interest and engagement with the subject has expanded the scope of the project and driven it from the outset. Our greatest debt of gratitude is to them.

Susan Ferleger Brades
Director, Hayward Gallery

Foreword

The collections held by the RIBA and V&A form the greatest holdings of architectural fact and fantasy in Great Britain. Both institutions began to collect prints, drawings and models at their foundations: the RIBA in 1834 and the V&A at its creation as the Museum of Manufactures in 1852. With a broad collecting policy, the RIBA has the largest number of artefacts – an estimated 600,000 drawings and 250 models.

The V&A, because historically its acquisitions guidelines have concentrated on design and exemplar works, has approximately 35,000 architectural drawings in its collections. However, whatever it might lack when comparing numbers of drawings with the RIBA, the V&A can boast enormous galleries filled with full-size casts of parts of famous buildings, whole original rooms taken from historic houses, and innumerable objects designed by architects: furniture, ceramics and glass, items of silver and gold, textiles and wallpapers, church furnishings, even doll houses – the list is a long one. So these two great collections, sometimes intentionally, sometimes accidentally, are very complementary to each other.

This year, the RIBA and the V&A will conclude the first part of a much closer relationship that has been developing over the last five years, entitled the V&A/RIBA Architecture Partnership. Whilst remaining wholly owned, run and staffed by the RIBA, its Drawings and Manuscripts Collections are moving to the V&A Henry Cole Wing, to be available to the public alongside the museum's prints, drawings and paintings. This exhibition, in collaboration with the Hayward Gallery's National Touring Exhibitions Programme, is the first major external manifestation of this new relationship between the museum and institute and draws on both collections.

There is little point in us as curators acquiring all these different objects unless we demonstrate why they are interesting and worth keeping to a wider public. Many of the drawings and models in *Fantasy Architecture* have never before been seen outside our study rooms and we are very grateful to Susan Ferleger Brades and her staff at the Hayward Gallery for the opportunity to show our collections outside London in the context of this timely and provocative exhibition.

Charles Hind
Assistant Director (Special Collections)
and Curator of Drawings
RIBA Library Drawings Collection

Introduction
Clare Carolin and Rob Wilson

The next time you walk a habitual route, or survey a familiar view, try this. Imagine that the past was different and that the future has already happened. Imagine that the urban fabric that surrounds you – the street under your feet, the passing vehicles, the skyline, the parks, the bridges, the cinemas, the cemeteries – are not what they are, but what they might have been, and could still be. If your visualisation is complete and effective you will be transported to the intangible world that coexists with the one you know. You will find yourself walking through, or gazing out at what the poet Wallace Stevens, contemplating an unexceptional evening in an ordinary place, once called 'the metaphysical streets of the physical town'.

As with any fantasy, the vision conjured will vary depending on the dreamer, and will draw on a complex array of other immaterial worlds known from drawings, books, films, newspapers and computer games. And as with any dream – or indeed any real town or city – scratch its surface and you will find more stories and images of forgotten events and inventions, ruined pasts, schemes to be completed, wishes to be fulfilled.

This book and the exhibition it accompanies have been conceived as an excavation of architecture's unrealised past and a means of shedding light on its future. In this context the terms 'fantasy' and 'architecture' are loosely interpreted: 'fantasy' embraces all forms of dreaming, from cursory 'back of the envelope' sketches to elaborate plans for fabulous new utopias drawn up in a spirit of romantic idealism; and 'architecture' to encompass almost every imaginable building type. These imagined buildings, structures and schemes are set in eight thematic groupings which reflect the recurrent images and forms of architectural fantasy throughout history. The first, *Private Worlds*, introduces the subject by equating the domestic setting – a place for dreaming – with mental space.

More so than any other art form, architecture is inextricable from the forces of politics, economics, social change and technological innovation. It feeds off these influences and in turn it helps drive them. Any history of fantasy architecture – however brief and circumscribed – will also be a history of the dreams and failures of the civilisation from which it emanates. The bulk of the material included in *Fantasy Architecture* is drawn from the RIBA and V&A Drawings Collections and is, in the main, a very European, not to say British, presentation of the subject, expressing Western preoccupations and events over centuries: the fascination with Classical culture; colonial expansion; the search for a national style; the Industrial Revolution; resistance to and infatuation with Modernism; post-war reconstruction; and counter-cultural outburst. By contrast, the recent work in *Fantasy Architecture*, which complements its precursors in type and spirit, reflects the current global concerns and workings of architecture, which have spawned new forms and expressions in response to contemporary realities and cultural obsessions.

Throughout the twentieth century architecture, the most public of the arts, and film, the most popular, have done much to enhance and reinforce each other's image. Film alone can simulate the experience of walking through architectural space, and architecture – real or virtual – can enhance any narrative. Recent developments in digital technology have transformed the depiction of the unbuilt world, putting moving imagery wholly at the disposal of architectural imagining and drawing artists and designers from other fields (whose work is also included here) into architectural fantasising. Stills and extracts from twentieth-century feature films, as well as computer-generated design simulations, are integrated throughout the various sections of *Fantasy Architecture*. And because inventing backdrops for spectacle, as well as designing spectacular buildings, has long been a preoccupation of architects, one section, *All the World's a Stage*, looks exclusively at architecture for, and as, theatre.

The historical remit of *Fantasy Architecture* is set by two points related to works included: 1500, the approximate date of the earliest drawing, an anonymous late-Medieval *Design for a tower with turrets* (cat.40); and 2036, the year in which the concluding scenes of William Cameron Menzies' 1936 film, *Things to Come*, are set (cat.87). In their use of reconstructed pasts, ruined presents and fantasy futures, these two works are characteristic anachronisms of fantasy architecture. The *Design for a tower*, with its crenellations, arrow-loops and gargoyles, reflects a romantic nostalgia and yearning back to a more chivalric age when buildings were made to withstand attack. Yet by virtue of its glazed frontage these glamorous military trappings would have been utterly useless in any real conflict and the tower and its occupants vulnerable. *Things to Come*, with sets designed by the artist Lázló Moholy-Nagy, offers a vision of the future from the past – an Art Deco-style hereafter, still yet to come.

Things to Come, and the novel by H.G. Wells on which it is based, further encapsulate the themes and elaborate the rationale for the groupings of *Fantasy Architecture*. Wells' description of the collapse and reconstruction of civilisation over centuries clearly demonstrates the relationship between a society and the buildings it creates and destroys – in reality as well as in dream. Moreover, the science fiction genre, itself an area of immense and growing importance to architectural fantasy, allows this relationship to be conveyed vividly. Analogous to *Fantasy Architecture* is *Historical Pictures*, described in Wells' novel as a book of documentary photographs and depicted in the film as a flat screen display for a child's lesson in architectural history. *Historical Pictures* shows the processes of a fictional history through images of actual architecture, 'the jumbling growths of the early phase of the twentieth century', and its future fantasy counterparts: completely new cities on green field sites; buildings designed for obsolescence; towering housing blocks set in parks; transportable dwellings and vast public clubs combining 'gymnastics and sports halls, dancing floors, conference rooms, the perpetual news cinema, libraries, reading-rooms, small studies, studios and social centres for reviving social life.'

Here, then, are prefigured the New Towns and *Urban Futures* of Clough Williams-Ellis (cat.135), Helmut Jacoby (cat.72) and Birds Portchmouth Russum Architects (cat.13); the disposable elements of Archigram's *Plug-In City* (cat.28); the *Megastructures* of Superstudio (cat.121, 122) and Constant (cat.27); Paolo Soleri's harmonious vision of architecture and ecology (cat.120); Foreign Office Architects' *Virtual House* (cat.44) – movable and infinitely adaptable to site; Cedric Price's *Fun Palace* (cat.105) and Zaha Hadid's *Peak Club* (cat.60), combining all social functions in a single complex. The accuracy with which fantasies of the future are predicted appears at first uncanny, and yet when we consider these more recent designs in the light of their historical precedents, certain paradigms of fantasy building-types start to crystallise. The earliest example of a movable house shown in this book dates from 1833 (cat.62) and the first megastructure from 1761 (cat.103). Wells' all-encompassing vision of a fully- automated utopia – the liberation of built form through technology – has long been a preoccupation of architectural fantasists, as the section *Appliance of Science* shows.

The last recorded event in the novel *The Shape of Things to Come* is 'the levelling of the remaining "skeletons" of the famous "Sky-scrapers" of Lower New York – the most old-fashioned city in the world.' In this instance science fiction fantasy fails to make an accurate forecast. As the section devoted to *Vertical Visions* attests, the ambition to make a statement by building a magnificent tower remains as potent today – even in the wake of the attacks on the World Trade Center of 11 September 2001 – as it was in the sixteenth century. Nevertheless, the imagined ruins of existing (or even proposed) buildings is a classic conceit of fantasy architecture – the staple of the architectural capriccio, witnessed here by the works included in *In Memoriam*, as well as the material in *Past Perfect*, which is devoted to the fascination for historic styles and attempts to envision ideal ancient worlds.

The very process of making, destroying and reconstructing worlds of building blocks is a game played by children from an early age and, in more sophisticated guise, by some adults. It is one that can be perpetually replayed through tools of the imagination, from wooden bricks to celluloid and now digital media. Of course real architecture only gets built, *as its designer intended*, when a dizzyingly complex set of circumstances conspire in its favour. Many of the designs in *Fantasy Architecture* were never meant to become reality but, like the cartoons of Louis Hellman (cat.64–68), or the works of Superstudio (cat.121, 122), are very deliberate polemical parodies of prevailing architectural fashions. Other proposals failed to make it off the drawing board because they were impractical, over-ambitious, flawed in their design or technically ahead of their time. Yet as construction techniques continue to evolve apace and nostalgia retains its powerful hold – as Peter Cook explains in his essay 'The Drawing as Wish' – some of these past fantasies might yet take concrete shape, just as the Channel Tunnel – once the dream of engineers, politicians and script-writers – has done already.

In a precipitously changing world many of us live in cities that we have seen expand and transform over the past decade. Global population explosion, mass migration and environmental degradation mean that space to build in the real world is shrinking. But with more of us equipped with the digitally-enhanced tools of dreaming and an urgent and growing need to find architectural solutions to contemporary problems, the world of architectural fantasy, and the means by which it is articulated through imagery, can only grow. If we can begin to interpret architecture's recurring dreams and nightmares they can serve to enrich and inform us – to guide our understanding of what has been lost or built in error and in so doing to benefit the shape of things to come.

On the Brink of a Tumultuous Abyss: Images of Fantasy and Visionary Architecture
Neil Bingham

Architectural fantasy, as a field of study with its own historical identity, emerged in the early 1960s with a small number of articles, books and exhibitions. Before this, little attempt had been made to identify the major figures and architectural movements of fantasy. Since then, not only has the subject become of broader interest, but written and visual histories of architectural fantasy have stimulated an ever-growing number of contemporary architects to design 'beyond architecture', in a manner departing from tradition.

Almost all researchers in this field generally agree that the terms 'fantasy' and 'visionary' are questionable and often indefinable labels that have become attached to designs that fall outside commonplace and work-a-day architecture. There is a debate as to whether it is possible to have built examples of fantasy and visionary architecture. An example often cited as 'built fantasy' is the *Einstein Tower* (fig.1) by the architect Eric Mendelsohn, a leading member of the Expressionist Movement. Opened in 1924, with its rounded, almost melting, profile, the building is nothing like any other observatory tower built before or since.

Nevertheless, it is generally accepted that fantastic and visionary architecture are at their best when presented as an illustration in any medium that allows the imagination to roam and shows the viewer the unexpected. Usually these images are on paper, or made into a three-dimensional model, or created for stage and film, or more popularly today, digitally imagined through the use of a computer.

'Fantasy' implies an architectural composition that is strange and unfamiliar to the eye, sometimes within the realms of possibility, but usually … fantastic. Beresford Pite's design for a gentleman's club in the centre of London, conjured up as a menacing Gothic castle (cat.104) is a fantasy: a deliberate exercise to amaze and amuse.

'Visionary' can be treated as a sub-division of fantasy, usually applied to designs of great scale and imagination, ahead of their time, often within the realms of possibility but, for whatever reason, not built. *The Great Victorian Way* of 1855 (cat.101), made by Sir Joseph Paxton, was a serious proposal for a ten-mile long covered arcade of shops, hotels and restaurants with an elevated railway. It was modelled on Paxton's very own iron and glass Crystal Palace, erected for the *Great Exhibition* of 1851 in London, which sceptics had scorned as unbuildable. An enthusiastic Prince Albert showed the drawing of *The Great Victorian Way* to Queen Victoria. Important politicians took up the cause. The scheme never got off the ground – in retrospect, we consider it as visionary.

In this relatively new field of discussion on fantasy and visionary, particular historical figures have emerged as influential leaders, architectural prophets who have pushed the limits of the imagination. As is to be expected, even between the great collections of the Royal Institute of British Architects (RIBA) and the Victoria and Albert

fig. 1
Eric Mendelsohn
Einstein Tower,
Potsdam, Germany
1924

fig. 2
Hugh Ferriss
'Looking west from
business center'
from *Metropolis
of Tomorrow*, 1929

fig. 3
Etienne-Louis
Boullée
*Project for a cenotaph
for Sir Isaac Newton,*
1784

1   2   3

Museum (V&A), not all of these fantastic and visionary architects are represented. There are no drawings, for example, by Hugh Ferriss, America's most celebrated architectural conjurer of ideal cities of the future, 1920s style (fig.2). However, it is a testimony of the strengths of the RIBA and V&A that there are not only good examples in the two collections by celebrated fantasists and visionaries, but examples by architects of superstar status. There are also works by the unsung and unknown heroes of the genre.

In the Valhalla of the visionary, the dreamland of fantasy, two figures tower over all others: Piranesi and Boullée. Master of dark, labyrinthine worlds, the Italian architect Giovanni Battista Piranesi has held a sustained and powerful position, influencing not only later visionary architects, but also practising architects as well as stage and set designers who have been charged by the strength of his evocative engravings. Piranesi was a superb etcher and engraver in copper and renowned for contrasting light and shadow. A Venetian by birth, he settled in Rome permanently in 1745 at the age of 20. Over the next 30 years, he published nearly 2,000 prints, mainly views of ancient Greek and Roman sites. But his most enduring work has been his suite of 16 prints, *Carceri d'Invenzione* (*Imaginary Prisons*, cat.103). With their sense of drama and romanticism – forbidding stone interiors crowded with bewildering staircases, bridges and arches – these images are still probably the best selling of all architectural facsimiles.

Unlike Piranesi's haunted world, the visionary architectural drawings of Etienne-Louis Boullée radiate optimism. In the turbulent decade leading to the French Revolution, between 1778 and 1788, Boullée created a series of drawings for public buildings and monuments as manifestations of his theory on the symbolic authority of architecture. Great architecture, he said, reflected the glory of Man, Nature and God. Boullée created extraordinary geometric forms, like his sphere-shaped funerary monument dedicated to Sir Isaac Newton (fig.3) and grand Neo-Classical temples worthy of the revolutionary new order. He presented these monuments of power as genuinely buildable proposals. Revolutionary France, however, was not prepared for such grandiose schemes.

Boullée's master drawing *Design for a Metropolitan Cathedral* (cat.14) comes from a set of drawings for a cathedral of omniscience. In an impassioned discourse on this scheme, Boullée spoke of the 'grandeur and majesty' of religious ceremonies as moments of profound reverence. Architecture, his architecture, was the catalyst. In its ecstasy, and eccentricity, Boullée's cathedral was to be used for one annual ceremony only – the Catholic feast of Corpus Christi, when the body of Christ, through the consecrated bread, is transfigured and displayed for adoration. This is the moment captured in the RIBA drawing. In this scene, the ceremony is dwarfed by the mighty architecture of thousands of columns, yet a radiance of unearthly light emanates from the high altar.

The Boullée drawing was given to the RIBA in 1838 as part of the first large and significant bequest from Sir John Drummond Stewart. Of Drummond Stewart's life we know little other than that he was a man of private means and an amateur architect. But he was obviously something of a dreamer because he was a diligent collector of fantasy drawings. Of the more than 100 drawings he presented, most were architectural capriccios and stage designs.

Amongst the Drummond Stewart collection is a substantial number of sheets by the Galli Bibiena family of artists who specialised in theatre designs on the Continent between the 1680s and 1780s (cat.50, 51, 52). In the drawings, as on stage, the Galli Bibienas created new architectural worlds. They were masters of perception, often employing several points of perspective to heighten the sense of space and distance. One of their favourite themes was palaces, heavenly buildings festooned with sculpture and encrusted with ornament, with grand staircases stretching in every direction and a seemingly unending flow of stately rooms.

The Galli Bibienas, like other designers and architects of their age, were often called upon to produce designs for ephemeral events – firework displays, triumphal arches and ceremonies. The temporary and usually celebratory nature of such occasions allowed these designers a high degree of imaginative freedom. In England during the early 1600s, Inigo Jones, the architect of the first Classical Renaissance buildings in Britain (the Banqueting House, Whitehall and the Queen's House, Greenwich), had also designed for such performances. As the favoured designer in the Stuart court, he created designs for masques, festivities and, more solemnly, funerals (cat.73).

By no coincidence, the provenance of many of the Inigo Jones drawings in the RIBA is the same as the most celebrated collection that the Institute holds, that by the Italian sixteenth-century architect Andrea Palladio. When travelling in Italy, Inigo Jones himself had acquired many of the Palladio drawings. In 1898, by descent, the 8th Duke of Devonshire gave the collection of more than 220 sheets in trust to the RIBA.

Included amongst these master works is Palladio's *Design for the Proscenium, Teatro Olympico, Vicenza, Italy* (fig.4). Similar, although a little more formal than the later Galli Bibienas, Palladio's theatrical setting was of course also illusory, a triumphal arch decorated with statues. However, Palladio's stage fantasy was to be frozen forever, his design not painted on canvas in the usual manner of theatre props, but built of wood and plaster (fig.5). It still stands today, used for its intended function.

Palladio's theatre in Vicenza forms a strong link to his reconstructions of ancient Roman buildings and sites. Like other Renaissance architects, Palladio looked to antiquity for sources and inspiration when creating his own architecture. He surveyed and sketched the majestic ruined buildings of ancient Rome. In the hillside remains at Praeneste, formerly called Palestrina, 35 miles east of the city of Rome, he found the muse who whispered to him of the glories of the past that could be even more glorious. Out of this crumbling complex of temples dedicated to the goddess Fortuna Primigenia, Palladio conjured up drawings of extraordinary flights of fantasy (cat.97). Based on archaeological observation, Palladio then fused his knowledge of other Roman temples and shrines as the medium for the enhanced transformation.

Archaeological reconstruction, even when attempting to reach historical accuracy, still relies upon the imagination of the artist to fill in the blanks. And that is where fantasy plays a large part. For example, three and a half centuries after Palladio, Henry Carlton Bradshaw had his go at reconstructing the ancient Roman temple complex at Praeneste (cat.15). It is almost difficult to believe, so astonishingly different is his interpretation from Palladio's, that the two architects had trod the same ground.

So many architects, having assiduously studied old ruins, were tempted into

fig. 4
Marc'Antonio
Palladio working
under the direction
of his father,
Andrea Palladio
*Design for the
Proscenium, Teatro
Olympico, Vicenza,
Italy, c.* 1579

recreating them on paper. Less academic and more interpretive and impressionistic than the Bradshaw are the studies by William Walcot. An architect, perspective artist and Classical scholar, Walcot specialised in black-and-white etchings and large and spectacular gouache paintings of ancient temples and sites. The gouaches are brightly coloured in accordance with the latest archaeological findings, and peopled with exotic figures (cat.130). Walcot was the inheritor of such well-known late-Victorian architect-artists as Henry William Brewer, a master of reconstructions who created astonishing panoramic views of medieval London and Paris for his own pleasure and that of the readers of *The Builder* magazine to which he regularly contributed (cat.16).

Plundering the past has long been a staple in the architectural repertoire. An extremely early, and rare, example is an English late-medieval drawing held by the RIBA for a palace or country house (cat.40). With its arrow loops and crenellated roofline, the building looks fortified, ready to withstand an attack. But like its gargoyles, this is all decorative romanticism, the fantasy of the past, giving this quiet domestic architecture and its occupants the aura of living in a brave chivalric era of knights and damsels, dungeons and dragons.

Often the past comes with a heavy dose of nostalgia, of lost loves and opportunities. When feeling nostalgic, we tend to embroider our memories, as did Sir John Soane when he became maudlin and self-pitying in his old age. His wife had died, he was at odds with his two sons, his eyesight failing. Although a highly respected and professionally successful architect, he began to dwell upon thoughts of his happier earlier years. One of the results was a painted composition of his initial unbuilt architectural works set in a romantic landscape, poignantly titled '*Architectural visions of early fancy in the gay morning of youth and dreams in the evening of life*' (cat.113 and fig.6). The young Soane wanders through his own world, walking in the shadow of death.

The mystery of the afterlife often elicits startling architectural evocations for the dead to dwell in. The RIBA and V&A are heavy with designs for tombs and temples, crematoriums and chapels, cemeteries and columbaria. The most visionary usually are on the grandest scale, like Seddon and Lamb's *Design for the Imperial Monumental Halls and Tower* (cat.108) and Thomas Harrison's *Design for a military and naval monument* (cat.61).

Yet even death can be played with, laughed at, as John Flaxman has done with his little sketch for a pompous tomb sprouting dismembered human limbs (cat.43). It is an irony that Flaxman's joke was at Soane's expense, poking fun at one of the very buildings that Soane was to include, half a century later, in his *Architectural visions of early fancy*. The object of Flaxman's little fantasy is in the top left corner, Soane's unbuilt mausoleum to his friend James King who had drowned when, as students, they had gone boating together.

fig. 5
Andrea Palladio
Proscenium of the Teatro Olympico, Vicenza, Italy, 1584

fig. 6
John Soane
Perspective by
J.M. Gandy
'*Architectural visions of early fancy in the gay morning of youth and dreams in the evening of life*', 1820

Architectural tall tales and white lies make for designs full of fun and enchantment. Thomas Affleck Greeves understood this; his *Design for a monument to commemorate the passing of the good old days of architecture* (cat.59) is a capriccio in the dotty style of Heath Robinson. Such eminent architects as Sir Edwin Lutyens and Sir Hugh Casson were also famous for their off-the-cuff caricatures. The letters Lutyens wrote to his friends, colleagues and clients, and especially to his wife – all of which are in the RIBA Manuscripts Collection – are peppered with witty parodies. The sketchbooks he created for Captain Day and, very poignantly, for his dying friend Barbara Webb, of houses that they could only dream over, were made to forget the harsh realities of this world (cat.77, 78). And isn't that what fantasy should do?

At the same time that Lutyens was throwing off his little humoresques, other architects were taking their fantasies much more seriously. The turbulence surrounding such momentous events as the First World War of 1914 to 1918 and the Russian Revolution of 1917 shook many architects into trying to bring order out of chaos. In this period, which harboured the rise of Modernism, several architectural movements became linked with a heightened sense of the imaginative in their search for new ideologies: in particular Russian Constructivism, Italian Futurism and German Expressionism.

The V&A recently purchased two fine Italian Futurist pieces by the architect Virgilio Marchi (cat.80, 81). These drawings visually articulate the polemical Futurist manifestos that proclaimed the scourging and re-foundation of society based on the new machine age. The architectural rallying cry had come from Antonio Sant'Elia, who had declared, 'We must invent and rebuild the Futurist city like an immense and tumultuous shipyard, agile, mobile and dynamic in every detail [...] It must soar up on the brink of a tumultuous abyss.' Marchi, a disciple of Sant'Elia, responded with his own vibrant city designs ordered on atypical architectural shapes and rushing patterns of urban traffic.

By the 1930s, modern architecture was still experimental, but in a less heated manner. The new leaders, such as Walter Gropius, Mies van der Rohe and Le Corbusier, sought rational, functional, uncompromising approaches to architecture and urban development. Even Eric Mendelsohn, a leading member of the 1920s Expressionists, had by the 1930s still retained his graceful line in both drawing and building design (cat.86), but was producing schemes as large and uncompromising as the other Modernists.

Following the Second World War, in the boom years in America and the period of reconstruction in Europe, it was these Modernists and their followers who made the greatest impact upon our towns and cities. Their methods, often didactic and empirical, are considered today by many critics as idealistic and utopian. In other words, another form of fantasy.

In Britain, these programmatic Modernists were given the opportunity to level and redesign whole sections of the country. Ernö Goldfinger was an early exponent of the new vision for the future (cat.56, 57), planning great series of high-rise flats during the Second World War which, when peace came, he was to build. Although many projects did not come to fruition, like Sir Leslie Martin's 1965 scheme to rebuild the government office buildings in Whitehall as one massive complex (cat.83), such a development was in the visionary tradition of Sir Charles Barry's similar attempt one hundred years earlier (cat.9).

By around 1960 there were scattered rumblings of rebellion against this prevailing mainstream Modernism. In Britain, Archigram was formed, a group of counter-culture architects designing on the brink of the unreal. Their schemes were for extraordinary projects such as cities and buildings made of components that can be plugged in, swung and floated into place and can even rise on large mechanical legs like giant insects. One can readily understand why they acknowledged a debt to the capsulated cities of their older American contemporary, Buckminster Fuller (cat.49, fig.7).

At the same time, in America, arose a scattered group of anti-establishment fantasy architects, especially prevalent in the mid-west, away from the conventions of the bigger centres. Frank Lloyd Wright, although mainstream, retreated to his desert winter camp, Taliesin West in Arizona, where he gathered around him, like a religious leader, his 'disciples'. Bruce Goff, in Oklahoma, produced eccentric architectural designs reliant upon natural materials. Also in Arizona, the Italian-born architect Paolo Soleri established his utopian community, Arcosanti, based on his concept of 'arcology': architecture and ecology in harmony (cat.120). Here, in an urban city, using solar power, there are to be no automobiles, the arcology so well designed that inhabitants are able to walk everywhere and be in touch with nature at the city's edge.

It was this generation, from the 1960s and early 1970s, of rebellious and free-thinking architects, alongside architectural critics and historians, that rediscovered and began to define the areas of fantasy and visionary architecture. At first they took up the historical movements of Expressionism and Futurism – largely ignored by architects of the Modern Movement – which they re-christened, for a short time, 'Fantastic Architecture'. There was a seminal exhibition in 1960 on 'Visionary Architecture' at the Museum of Modern Art, New York. The movement gathered momentum, as a new generation of fantasy architects arose, such as of the Italian group Superstudio (cat.121, 122), whose 'conceptual' architectural schemes of futuristic cities were firmly in the historical tradition of Hugh Ferriss and Buckminster Fuller. Even the mainstream Post-Modern movement during this period, which witnessed Modernism blending Classical elements with an ironic twist, had a playful pretence of historical fantasy about it.

Today, the architectural world of fantasy proliferates, aided by the technological wizardry of the computer. With a strong tradition behind them, the new fantasists, like their historic predecessors, reach beyond everyday building to transfigure, distort, extend and give new meanings to architecture.

fig. 7
Buckminster Fuller
Design for a hemispherical environmental dome, two miles in diameter, showing how it would enclose a large part of New York City: aerial view, 1968

Fighting the Banalities of the Built: Pop Capriccios, Visionary Videos and Beyond
Rob Wilson

Over the last few years, a new boldness, bravura even, not seen since the 1960s, has returned to architectural design and its depiction. Ideas and proposals for unbuilt, indeed often unbuildable, structures are being produced not just by architects but by many others working in different visual media – film designers, advertising creatives, music video producers, fine artists and computer-game programmers – reflecting both the general cultural climate and a new-found appetite for fantasy architecture.

The dominance of the visual in our increasingly image-led culture has been driven largely by the development of digital technology. This has facilitated instant global access, transfer, manipulation and reproduction, enabling new ways of imaging and imagining. As a result, the imagery of unbuilt architecture has become more sophisticated at aping the 'true' photographic image, whilst simultaneously becoming more ubiquitous and disposable. Building proposals or reconstructions are now difficult to distinguish from the records of existing ones (cat.90), with the image becoming an end in itself.

In today's media-saturated environment, many of these depictions of possible architectures have been designed for mass consumption: they face us daily on advertising hoardings, on television screens, in newspapers and magazines, and in cinemas. But why this sudden abundance of architectural imagery?

Recently, there has been a huge increase in public interest, knowledge and appetite for contemporary architectural design. This has been fuelled in countries such as Britain by ever more ambitious TV makeover programmes, which have expanded their remit from sofa colours to roof structures. As part of modern hyper-consumer culture, unbuilt buildings and structures are being increasingly depicted as environments to sell 'total lifestyle experience' – not just as aspirational images, but as spaces created as reflections of the self. This trend was parodied and epitomised by the series of projects created by Softroom for *Wallpaper** magazine (cat.114–118), whose bi-line defined an era: 'the stuff that surrounds you'.

Images of fantasy architecture have also found a growing role in future plans for new city centres and public buildings and spaces – gauging public reaction to planned developments and regeneration projects. This reflects a recent global building boom spurred on by the explosion of new 'signature' buildings with which many cities and countries chose to mark the Millennium. Other notable examples include the various schemes proposed to replace the World Trade Center towers after the terrorist attacks of 11 September 2001. The initial proposals for the redevelopment of the site were uninspired arrangements of tower blocks whose collective size was generated solely by the minimum requirements for lettable office space. These met with luke-warm public reaction, particularly in the light of other unofficial but far more imaginative design

fig. 8
Johann Bernhard Fischer von Erlach *Perspective view of Solomon's Temple* from *A plan of civil and historical architecture*, 1725

fig. 9
Pieter Bruegel the Elder *Tower of Babel*, 1563

8

9

proposals – such as Foreign Office Architects' design for a group of sinuous towers (cat.45). The competition that followed, with seven competing architectural firms – including Foster and Partners, who proposed a scheme for two 'kissing towers' (cat.47) – was inevitably subject to intense media and public scrutiny. Digital images of the different proposals for the iconic downtown Manhattan skyline were reproduced in news reports and design magazines worldwide, stimulating global debate.

Atmospheric and suggestive designs such as those produced for the Millennium and the World Trade Center are typical of what makes for great fantasy architecture: a celebration of the imaginative power and skill of the designer and the representation of the project in a single image. Crucially, fantasy architecture must engage the imagination of the viewer with imagery that is not over-proscriptive, leaving them the space in which to project their own narratives and imagined futures, particularly pertinent with a project as emotionally charged as the redevelopment of the World Trade Center site.

Whatever the technical innovations in the processes of representation, it is important to stress the continuity of cultural influences, of fact and fiction, from which the designs and images of the unbuilt draw their inspiration. The legendary, lost or ruined structures of history – the labyrinth of Daedalos, Nero's Golden House, William Beckford's Fonthill Abbey, Joseph Paxton's Crystal Palace – still haunt and provide cues for fantasy architecture. From Solomon's Temple of Jerusalem (fig.8) to Asymptote's *New York Stock Exchange* (cat.8), vast and complex structures still embody power – whether of religion or money. Similarly, the Tower of Babel (fig.9) provides a cautionary tale for all tower-builders, including the architect Howard Roark in the film *The Fountainhead* (cat.128), of the ultimate futility of human ambition. The potential for hubris represented by towers stretching to the heavens still provides a constant reminder for every project aiming to be the 'tallest in the world' (cat.46).

By its very precision of description yet obliqueness to the visual, literature has also inspired the designs of imagined spaces – be it Dante Alighieri's *Divine Comedy* for the design premise of Guiseppe Terragni and Pietro Lingeri's *Danteum* in Rome (cat.91) or Friedrich Dürrenmatt's play *The Physicists* as inspiration for a villa designed by Eric Parry (cat.99).

As in the case of the World Trade Center, buildings can themselves become news, but more often they are associated with, or symbolise, events. Today's obsession of the media with fame, conspiracy theories and the cult of celebrities who die young, is nothing new and has often provided the narratives that inspire designs. For example, the *Princess Diana Memorial Bridge* by FAT (cat.42), which incorporates a slice of the countryside where the late Princess is buried, echoes the inspirations for the design of other memorial structures going back to the Canopus at Hadrian's Villa. The Canopus, with its elaborate water features and Egyptian details, was constructed as a representation of the source of the Nile, in which the Emperor Hadrian's lover had drowned in mysterious circumstances. The ruins of this structure and the rumours surrounding it have in turn inspired Piranesi, Rossini and Le Corbusier (fig.10). The Canopus is also an example of how, even in Imperial Roman times, Egypt was already associated with secret knowledge, curses and mystery. This link inspires the fantasy backdrops to horror films and video games to this day (cat.2).

The World Trade Center is only one example of a recent resurgence in high-profile architectural competitions involving world-class architects. This has been spurred by the success of architectural projects such as the Guggenheim Museum in Bilbao by Frank Gehry, which attracted worldwide attention and investment into the city – a building that has become an icon of urban renaissance and regeneration. The competition process has required architects to produce more accessible images of their proposals, not as blueprints for construction, but in order to win over competition assessors. Increasingly, these proposals are being used as tools to engage with the myriad of different people, including stakeholders and interest groups, that are part of the often mandatory public consultations on new projects.

Recently, there has been a trend away from the design of 'signature' buildings – particularly in Britain, where a number of so-called Millennium projects, funded by the National Lottery, have come to be seen as white elephants, isolated from the environments and communities in which they are situated. Many architectural projects today are for masterplans, whole areas of cities that integrate a range of functions. Designs for masterplans need to show the overall structure of a project, giving a sense of individual buildings and public space without using too high a level of detail. They are inspirational frameworks for a town's future and provide the perfect ingredients for visionary, architectural imagery. In Birds Portchmouth Russum's collage rendering of *Croydon, The Future* (cat.13), for example, a string of multi-storey carparks is transformed into a series of colourful inflatable structures providing spaces for sports arenas, cinemas and pop concerts.

The designs for this scheme illustrate the elements of showmanship and playfulness found in many a *tour-de-force* of architectural draughtmanship. Often these exist solely as bravura exercises of virtuosity, or illustrations of a private whim or fancy, in the tradition of the architectural capriccio. Capriccios can inspire both feelings of pleasure but also of shock and uncertainty, as Geoff Shearcroft's genetically modified mouse exemplifies (cat.110).

The designs of many recent contemporary schemes often seem to risk appearing quirky or gimmicky in order to catch attention, but this could equally be seen as a welcome return of the eighteenth-century concept of *jeu d'esprit* to architectural representation. This term refers to a wit and lightness of touch combined with a facility and mastery of the medium through which it is represented – be it pen and wash or computer-generated imagery.

In his introductory essay to the catalogue for *Flights of Fantasy* in 1986, an exhibition at the Clarendon Gallery in London of mainly eighteenth-century architectural capriccios, Jeremy Howard identified this playfulness in the tacked-on historical details found in many Post-Modern designs of the time. From today's perspective, much Post-Modern architecture now seems the opposite: a joyless exercise crudely referencing some mythic past, papering over a lack of positive social vision or purpose since the perceived failure of the Modern movement. This 'failure', memorialised in Tom Mellor's *Capriccio of Notre-Dame du Haut, Ronchamp, France in ruins* (cat.85), was predicated on the very success experienced by Modern movement architects who, from post-war reconstruction up to the 1960s, had been offered amazing opportunities to propose (cat.83) and even build their own versions of utopia. This exposed many untested designs to all the inevitable pitfalls of applying a vision to reality: the devil is in the detail. In the rush to construct, many mistakes were made, not least failing to get the views of the people who were expected to live in these brave new worlds – hence the mania of consultation today.

There was an immense optimism in the late 1950s and early 1960s, echoed in the years immediately preceding the Millennium, based on a belief in the possibilities of new technology to transform not only buildings and cities but societies too. This period saw a flowering of fantasy architecture with projects such as Archigram's *Plug-In City* (cat.28). This design proposed a continually evolving structure with parts that could be disposed of and replaced once their use had been fulfilled: the exact opposite of a utopian vision. Indeed, Archigram drew inspiration for these projects from sources in popular culture, such as American comic books, rather than architecture. As Peter Cook commented in 1967, 'The pre-packaged lunch is more important than Palladio.'

The dream of technology and automation was also central to the artist Constant's ideas and his project for an ideal city, *New Babylon* (cat.27), which, like Archigram's *Plug-In City*, is a megastructure. This architectural conceit, so beloved of 1960s visionaries, takes the form of a single structure that combines all of the functions of a city. In direct opposition to the Modernist tenet 'form follows function', Constant proposed that this megastructure be formed of endless inter-linking 'ludic' spaces – for free-play – where people could enjoy eternal leisure. In the UK, Cedric Price's scheme for a *Fun Palace* in East London (cat.105) was inspired by similar ideas. This massive open structure was designed to be flexibly programmed, with mobile spaces for dance, drama and music – 'a laboratory of fun' – and no doubt wall-to-wall *jeu d'esprit*! This project would later prove influential on the design of the Centre Pompidou (1971–77) in Paris by Richard Rogers and Renzo Piano. Conceived as a 'giant climbing frame', its exposed framework was originally designed to enable elements to be continually changed and replaced as required.

In contrast, it was the Modernist tendency to represent visionary structures of the future as pure and Cartesian but often unpopulated, essentially inhuman and monumental in scale, that was critiqued by Superstudio in their *Continuous Monument* series (cat.121). Here, the idea of the megastructure is taken to its literal and absurd extreme. Its structure extends across the whole planet – all *jeu d'esprit* squeezed out – completely inappropriate in scale and impermeable to the everyday world that it was meant to transform.

By 1970, when Constant abandoned the *New Babylon* project, megastructures had been condemned as 'chimera of utopia' by Utopie – a Marxist collective of architects, urban theorists and sociologists including Jean Baudrillard – at the conference *Utopia and/or Revolution* in Turin. Two years later, megastructures were pronounced 'dead' by the architectural historian Reyner Banham. By then the student protests that had originated in Paris in May 1968 had already failed to spark revolution against the existing social order in countries such as France. But perhaps more symbolically, the Moon landings from 1969 onwards, seeming to herald a new space age, actually initiated a period of introspection. The astronauts' view back to a suddenly fragile-looking 'blue planet' ushered in an era not of daring and brave new worlds but of risk aversion, fear of liability and a retreat into an idea of the past, not the future. Projects such as the Poundbury extension to Dorchester in the UK, masterplanned by Leon Krier for Prince Charles, were predicated on the dream of village greens and maypoles rather than that of 'ludic' space. Meanwhile, NASA's projections of an American mid-western suburbia on a space station remained resolutely in the realms of fantasy (cat.92).

With architects so busy struggling to build fragments of utopia, film became the main dream-tool for fantasy architecture for much of the twentieth century. From the 1920s onwards, the forms of Modernist architecture were very influential on film set design. In *Der Golem* (cat.132), the Expressionist architect Hans Poelzig created the complex, organic spaces that form its backdrops, whilst the cityscapes in *Just Imagine* (cat.18) were inspired by the work of the architect Raymond Hood and the architectural delineator Hugh Ferriss (fig.2). Through films such as these, the forms of Modern architecture were popularised to a mass audience. Whilst the seminal 1932 exhibition *Modern Architecture: International Exhibition* at the Museum of Modern Art in New York was seen by 33,000, the weekly average attendance at American cinemas had reached 85 million by the end of the 1930s.

The initial employment of stage techniques, such as painted backdrops, for film set design gradually gave way to the use of sophisticated models, which enabled filmmakers to combine a sense of scale with that of movement and spatiality on the big screen. Unconstrained by practicalities, fantasy film architecture could realise Modernist designs on a scale impossible in the real world – most famously in Fritz Lang's 1927 silent film *Metropolis* (fig.11), in which we see a vast mechanised city run by a down-trodden underclass. This film exemplified a growing tendency in the cinema to represent cities of the future in a negative light, identifying the ideological imposition of Modernist architecture with authoritarianism.

In 1982, Ridley Scott's *Blade Runner* fixed a new, iconic dystopian vision of the city, reiterated in films like Wim Wenders' *Until the End of the World* of 1991 (cat.133). In both films, the cities are based on real ones – Los Angeles and Paris respectively – presenting incomplete utopian visions, ad-hoc and provisional. Indeed it is the frenetic, dirty human mess of the old city streets with which the viewer is ultimately compelled to empathise – contrasted with the soulless quiet of the vast, light-drenched fantasy architectural forms of the Tyrell Corporation's pyramids or Jean Nouvel's *Endless Tower*, which loom above.

Today, big-budget films use digital techniques to realise imaginary buildings and cities in incredible complexity – or re-create them. So overwhelming is the use of computer-generated detail seen in films such as Peter Jackson's *Lord of the Rings* trilogy (2001–03) that it has been criticised by some reviewers as leaving no imaginative space for the audience.

In contrast, outside the necessarily all-enveloping world of the cinema, depictions of fantasy architecture using simpler digital techniques are often just as skillful but subtler in their effect. The work of Hayes Davidson, continuing in the rich tradition of architectural perspectivists and renderers such as Henry Brewer (cat.16) and Helmut Jacoby (cat.72), shows projections of future buildings and cities that have an almost dreamlike quality. In their short animation *Fast Forward* (cat.63), supposedly everyday snapshots of London are presented, but famous landmarks have been repositioned, jostling with huge new structures shimmering on the horizon. These images, designed to test the viewer's visual memory, have the unsettling frisson of the strangely familiar.

It has only been in recent years that the computer has finally bedded-down as just another design and image-making tool for architects themselves. There was a tendency to see a discontinuity in representation between it and previous mediums: 'machine-made' computer-aided design and digitally manipulated images contrasted with that of the 'hand' – of pencil and pen. But it was only the skill to manipulate this new tool that was lacking. Computers, once associated with the dumbing-down of design and

fig. 10
Le Corbusier
Sketch of the Canopus at Hadrian's Villa, Tivoli, Italy, 1910

fig. 11
Fritz Lang
Metropolis, 1927
(still)

fig. 12
Hieronymous
Bosch
The Garden of Earthly Delights,
c. 1500
(central panel)

10

11

12

of dreaming – useful only for space planning and reducing architecture to the lowest common denominator – are now equally used to sketch and roughly block-out designs, as well as to produce highly finished presentation images (cat.126).

However, it is not for their technical but their imaginative skills that architects and designers are in demand across more and more fields – creating new fantasy architectures for stock exchanges (cat.8) and pop princesses (cat.119) – celebrating the possibilities but also warning against the constraints of digital techniques. The designs of the buildings themselves are also influenced by digital technologies, which produce forms that were fantastical if not impossible a few years ago. Some of these are still to be built, as with the work of Greg Lynn (cat.79) or Will Alsop (cat.4): fantasy can become fact. With their role and remit expanding, architects are again looking outwards for inspiration for their fantasy architecture. Buildings as organisms are back with new, intricate structures echoing natural forms – for instance, Greg Lynn's *Ark of the World* project (cat.79).

In the 1990s, the progress of technology seemed to turn inwards, away from the Space Age, towards nano-technology, bio-technology and cloning: unraveling the spirals of DNA, not the Solar System. In the place of the mammoth exuberance of Ron Herron's *Walking City* (cat.69), we have Geoff Shearcroft's scurrying house-mouse (cat.110). With the focus back on the individual, Constant's world of leisure seemed to triumph in the 1990s not as a communal but as a consumerist ideal, with people reverting to the private spaces of their pampered lives – witnessed by Softroom's projects for *Wallpaper** magazine (cat.114–118), and engaging in the virtual interaction of games like *SimCity*™ (cat.37). This game, in which you can create, build, run and destroy your ideal city, demonstrates how the simultaneous miniaturisation of the circuit board and the digital world of the computer has given new scope to evoke vast dreams – but of virtual megastructures, inside the hard drive. Ironically, Asymptote's virtual *New York Stock Exchange* (cat.8), a spatial representation of the flows of global capitalism, exhibits the flexibility of structure of Constant's *New Babylon* (cat.27), but represents the triumph not of a new society but of the power of private Tyrell-like corporations. Appropriately for a megastructure of Mammon, the architects were inspired by the landscapes of Hieronymous Bosch's sixteenth-century painting *The Garden of Earthly Delights* (fig.12).

Today, with the virtual failing, so far at least, to deliver a perfect simulacrum of actual experience, the focus seems to be shifting outwards again – it is perhaps no coincidence that space stations on the Moon and landings on Mars are back on NASA's agenda. It is this very failure of the virtual – the digital image remaining as representation not reality – that reinforces its role as a tool of the imagination. It emphasises the stand-alone power of images themselves and has contributed to the revival of the art of the capriccio and the role of fantasy architecture today.

This underlines how the built environment we inhabit is just the residue of a much greater imaginative world that never saw the light of day, evoking what might have been or still could be – the unbuilt, the lost, the ephemeral and the future. We cling to the small visible tip of a gigantic submerged iceberg of fantasy, which itself provides enduring imaginative sustenance against the banalities of the built.

The Drawing as Wish
Peter Cook

In a way, all architecture can be fantasy. What distinguishes the values and aspirations of good and imaginative architecture from the world of building construction? The former can choose any medium, any technique, and can tell any story it likes. Colour and atmosphere can be conjured-up by pictorial techniques and tricks of the pen: the architect-artist can depict what he or she wishes might happen. But on the building site there are pragmatic, cause-and-effect aspects of construction that are fed by diagrams that, by definition, should leave nothing to the imagination. Today it is possible to load a whole pile of factual requirements, cost and site conditions, and timetables and – via the computer – produce a 'ded-sign' for a building based upon data. What will have happened to that whole set of myths, rituals, gambits and symbols that give delight through the intermixing of ideas and of references? Such indulgence (if that is what it is) or culture (more likely) has been prompted by a collective memory system we should refer to as architectural *mannerism*. Such a culture incorporates values and symbols drawn from a wide range of sources and interprets them with wit.

Of course, parallels exist outside architecture. A politician preparing for a speech, a pupil preparing for an exam, a teenager preparing for a date – they will all resort to a progressive sequence of predictions and paranoias through which they will imagine the circumstances of the ultimate event. They will fear disappointment; they will aim for survival and recognition. Only with confidence and success will they begin to relax. Eventually, if all goes well, they may become more and more audacious. Meanwhile, they may well have all indulged in that psychological construct of 'if only' and will have devised for themselves some idealised scenario. Indeed, they will have fantasised.

The architectural process is not an abstract. It has its basis in life as much as in myth. The politician may dream of a perfect, manipulable proletariat, the pupil of a ridiculously easy examination, the teenage boy of a lascivious encounter with a goddess. So the architect will dream of a perfect client, an ideal site and an endless budget. Of materials that shine or bend or draw blood (depending on taste). Of structures that float on air or reach deep into the underworld.

If only the politician, pupil or teenager had access to another palliative – another means of reaching towards a reality that still does not have to be reality. And here, for once, the architect can have an immense advantage in his or her ability to draw. Like a dream, a drawing does not have the same strictures as a building. It is distanced from the real and can take advantage of this. The appetite can be whetted and drawings can generate wishes (almost) requited. Drawing breaks through barriers: 'so the sun isn't blue … so what?'

The issue soon becomes fascinatingly, gorgeously complex: where does the drawing stand in relation to one's first idea? Second thoughts? Deliberate simplification? Deliberate elaboration? Deliberate accumulation of architectural symbols? Sometimes losing the plot in the process! As a teacher, I certainly know about that last one. The clever student will often load a drawing with too many tantalising visual messages that say, 'Look … I know that one and that one and that one, don't I? … Look, I've reinterpreted Lutyens or something from *The Matrix*.'

Almost every moment in the documented history of architectural ideas suggests to us that the person drawing was aware of an audience. Some wonderful architects have been content to just scribble the latest detail of a window or a staircase on the nearest available piece of wood or newly-laid plaster with only the carpenter as audience. Nowadays, they are content to email a description of the components required and their time-sequence. Frank Gehry (designer of the Guggenheim Museum in Bilbao and the recently completed Disney Concert Hall in Los Angeles) is certainly too eager and full of ideas to wait for the intricate process of making elegant drawings. He gets his assistants to make large models, which he will then circulate around the office, adding-on pieces or taking them off: working as a sculptor and then, only if really necessary, making some rough scribbles on paper. The final models are then 'tracked' by C3D computer and electronically turned into drawings (and, in some cases, turned directly into material cutting programmes). The results are hardly pragmatic or unimaginative: so it might be argued that today we can have architectural visions conceived without drawing.

Nonetheless, it still seems appropriate to relate the craftiness and earthy Romanticism of Frank Lloyd Wright to pencil or, even better, to the cragginess of his pencil-crayon. When you push or drag that slightly brittle and reluctant material along the paper, there is a certain issue of 'orchestration' involved: just as the Cor Anglais can be selected as the ideal instrument for the nuance of a particular melody, so a crisply drawn ink can create the perfect reference to a particular architectural detail.

Hand drawing has provided many opportunities for the intentional to be played against the cogitative: drawing speed is not always an advantage. This 'difficult' process provides time to think. Imagine the time there would be to think if you were scratching away at all the little lines that would, eventually, add up to the panoramic etching of a whole façade. Compare that with the wonderful combination of urge and surge of Lebbeus Woods rasping his pen or pencil across the page. More than any other late-twentieth-century drawings, those of this New York-based architect have inspired younger architects. None of his own buildings exist (though he did work on built buildings in his youth), yet the combination of realistic detail, bold form, atmospheric colour and texture combine to suggest that they really could exist. Woods is the contemporary master of gesture and reality in drawing – vision and likelihood. Somehow he is able to feed into his drawings a series of mannerisms that acquire bits and pieces, funny little objects, hints of patina, even 'spookiness', if necessary.

Another inspirational figure is Walter Pichler. Never formally trained as an architect, he has made series of drawings that (as well as his sculpted objects) explore the mysterious interface between animal skeletons, urban armatures, decay and geometry – preoccupations that are also often to be found in the work of Austrian artists. Somehow Pichler's drawings bring together aspects of spirituality, surface, decay and the fundamentals of structure – it is weird, but powerful stuff. Some of his mannerisms are repeated in the drawings of his contemporaries: Hans Hollein, Gunther Domenig and Raimund Abraham, key figures of the late-twentieth-century scene. Renowned makers of original work such as Michael Webb (one of the founders of Archigram) and Peter Wilson – both of whom have had a profound effect on younger architects by way of their drawn architecture – frequently invoke Pichler's work. Pichler's extreme actions involve such things as physically attacking a sheet of paper in preparation for a drawing – he will scrunch-up a dense sheet of Schoellerhammer (the densest and toughest German drawing paper) leaving a virtual 'crater' in the surface and will then enjoy the subsequent inconsistency of that surface as he works over it with the drawing.

Peter Wilson's own work of the 1970s and 1980s is imbued with a special atmosphere of poetic 'sweetness' that he and his wife, Julia Bolles, managed to transfer onto their breakthrough building, the Munster City Library (1985–93). Hans Hollein has also managed the same transition with his Municipal Museum Abeiberg in Moenchengladbach (1972–82). In both cases, the drawn nuance has much to do with the state of the drawn project: its materiality, its mood, its softness or hardness. So shape, though definitive, is almost trailing behind as a statement.

Lebbeus Woods and Michael Webb both create a brilliant mythical situation on their pieces of paper: if Woods can make you believe that the unlikely is likely, Webb can juxtapose objects derived from his Cushicle or Suitaloon (which are highly technologic personal enclosures) against dream-like landscapes and notions of evacuated space. The drawings of his Temple Island project have become apocryphal statements among architectural theorists and architects of all shades who graphically invent or indulge. Drawing was the only possibility for him to develop such juxtapositions and after years of lectures and exhibitions he continues to work back and forth over two or three reiterated themes from the safety of a quiet town in upstate New York. His Sin Centre, an early and more overt piece, also provides sustenance for the new work.

These architects can seemingly pitch a drawing at almost any point in the scale of normality or fantasy, even deciding that they will not recognise the divide between. Maybe it is simple: the so-called 'fantastic' architect is just the one who has pushed a little bit further than the 'ordinary' architect. Good buildings are pretty 'fantastic' because they are rare. Many 'fantastic' buildings should have been built.

The celebration of drawings has thus a more critical role *vis-à-vis* architectural progress than it is often credited. Yet in celebrating 'drawn-only' architecture, by suggesting (as one must) that some drawn-only architecture has a power and vision that escapes the everyday, there is always the danger that we will become too comfortable with its convenient separation from the day-to-day business of building. Such separation can be viewed as a useful way of dealing with things – particularly in England where eccentric ideas are deftly tolerated and simultaneously ignored – or as establishing an impotent territory of the 'fantastic' or the 'visionary' where some good ideas that might seem a bit odd can be politely kept aside from the business-in-hand.

From a personal point of view, I get a special kick from building something such as the recently completed *Kunsthaus in Graz* (Peter Cook and Colin Fournier, 2003, fig.13). A shining blue bubble with 1,000 pixilated fluorescent points of light that play pictures back at the city, with tubes reaching out to the sky and giant pins of structure darting out into space: the kind of building that everybody had expected to stay just as a fantasy scheme – yet I can report that (to me) the reality seems far more fantastic than the drawings!

fig. 13
Peter Cook and
Colin Fournier
Kunsthaus in Graz,
2003

13

Plates

Private Worlds

96.
ORA-ÏTO (est. 1998)
10,000Hz Legend – Air, 2001 (detail)

Parisian design group ORA-ÏTO began
their operation with an online catalogue,
which was used to publicise ironic virtual
buildings and products parodying the latest
trends in architecture, fashion and design.
In stark contrast to their 'branded
buildings' and dystopic visions of Paris in
2010 invaded by multinational brands,
this image shows a design for a virtual
home commissioned by French pop group
Air as artwork for the cover of their album
10,000Hz Legend. It is one of a series of
images of the fictional setting in which the
band, cut off from the world, supposedly
record and broadcast their music. The
House of Legend, with its vast cantilevered
room, is a kind of musical observatory
equipped with a huge satellite dish to
receive and transmit 10,000Hz radio
airwaves as well as all the equipment
required to produce Air's electronic music.

Private Worlds

5.
Anchor Blocks; F.A.D. Richter & Co.
(Rudolstadte, Thuringia, Germany)
Anchor Blocks, c. 1920s
Book of designs for Anchor Blocks No. 206:
Bungalow Box, c. 1920s
Book of designs for Anchor Blocks No. 208:
Suburban Box, c. 1920s

From the early 1880s to the 1920s, Anchor
building sets, made by Richter (reputably
the world's oldest toy manufacturer), were
the most popular construction toy in the
world. They came in many variations. This
set is aimed at the British middle class
market, with its suburban and bungalow
models; and, in the post-First World War
era, the *Made in Germany* is kept in very
small type. The box cover emphasises that
the enjoyment and fantasy experienced
through building toys never loses its magic,
no matter how old you become.

24.
Max Clenndining (b. 1934)
Perspective by Ralph Adron
Design for an interior, made for The Daily
Telegraph *newspaper*, 1968

The architect Max Clenndining has been
an influential creator of domestic interiors
and furniture, especially during the 1960s
and 1970s. In 1968, he was one of several
designers commissioned by the editor
of *The Daily Telegraph* for a spread in the
newspaper's colour supplement entitled
'Take a room'. In this Pop-style drawing
made by the theatre designer Ralph
Adron, Clenndining shows the editor and
his wife in their psychedelic home. The
architect believed that 'everything should
be the same colour, like sculpture, with a
unity between furniture and room.'

44.
Foreign Office Architects (est. 1992)
Virtual House, 1997

This scheme was devised as an entry for a
competition run by *ANY* magazine and the
firm Franz Schneider Brackel. The
competition was based on the premise that:
'the world that is best is the most "multiple"
one, the most virtual one.' The brief was
for a house with 200 square metres of floor
space, four rooms, each with an outdoor
space and maximum flexibility of form,
function and site. Composed of continuous
interlocking surfaces, forming floors,
walls and roofs, this 'virtual' house can be
located literally anywhere: from dense
woodland to arid desert.

55.
German (maker unknown, probably
made in Munich)
'Moderne Baukunst', c. 1830s–40s

This early set of manufactured toy blocks
is based on the principal of a non-
interlocking jigsaw. On the box lid, a figure
of Architecture, in the heroic form of the
goddess Athena, directs a group of *putti*
in excavating antique ruins, indicating
to the playing child that good architecture
is based upon historical precedent. The
picture blocks and accompanying leaflets
taught the child the basic Classical and
Gothic styles. Mixing the two styles may not
have looked or been considered correct,
but was definitely part of the fun.

57.
Ernö Goldfinger (1902–87)
*Drawing showing a typical modern type
of urban flat*, 1942

In this happy scene, the future seems
bright and modern despite the war raging
at the time. Goldfinger produced this
drawing for publication in an issue of the
Architectural Review on 'Planning for the
Future'. Its rigid structure and formality
lies firmly in the universal truths on town
planning that were beginning to dominate
the period, especially through the
polemics of Le Corbusier.

67.
Louis Hellman (b. 1936)
A Palace for a Premier, 2003

This is one of a series of 'Cele-buildings'
designed by architect-turned-cartoonist
Louis Hellman to reflect the egos of their
owners. In plan they are portraits that
can only be viewed by the super rich and
powerful as they ascend and descend
in helicopters. The idea for the series
developed from Hellman's earlier project,
'Archi-têtes': portraits of famous architects
in their signature building styles.
As Hellman explains, 'the idea for the
Archi-têtes grew from an interest in
anthropomorphism in architecture,
the idea that buildings are like faces and
bodies. They have façades. The whole
vocabulary of architecture is related to
the human form.'

126. (top)
Ushida Findlay (est. 1998)
Design for Grafton New Hall, 2001

119. (bottom)
Softroom (est. 1994)
Lollyworld, 1999

This design reworks the theme of the English country house for twenty-first-century living in response to contemporary social and environmental needs. Set on a 114 acre estate in Cheshire, the orientation and mass of Grafton New Hall is informed by the location, with its low-level design blending with the landscape. Radiating limbs accommodate guest bedrooms, a swimming pool and a cinema. The orientation and arrangement of the interior spaces is determined by the position of the sun at the time when each space is likely to be used.

The virtual homeworld of Lolly, a popstar manufactured to appeal to eight to twelve year olds, *Lollyworld* was the setting for the single released from *My First Album*, which was a top ten music video. Conceived as an 'Alice in Wonderland' style environment, *Lollyworld* operates on two scales. First, it is a handheld box of tricks that fits into Lolly's 'Lollypocket', which she wears as a belt. Second, it is a private world into which she can retreat. The architectural promenade it contains comprises her villa in a walled garden, a bed tower, underground control room, magic extending catwalk, pool and skating-rink.

Private Worlds

93.
Christopher Nicholson (1904–48)
Perspective by Hugh Casson (1910–99)
Design for the living room for the Pantheon,
West Dean, West Sussex, 1938

The Second World War intervened
before the wealthy collector of Surrealist
art, Edward James, could erect a country
house, the Pantheon, reusing an
eighteenth-century façade of a London
assembly hall. At another of his houses,
Monkton, James had asked Nicholson and
Casson to design the living room, as Casson
recalled, 'like the insides of an unhealthy
dog, panting in an uneven way.' In 1939,
James, an eccentric millionaire, moved to
the Mexican jungle where he hand-built a
concrete fantasy of towers and spires.

77.
Edwin Lutyens (1869–1944)
'Castle-in-the-air' sketchbook, showing an
imaginary palace entitled 'Port Fleuviale de
Circonstance', c. 1895–96

Lutyens was an established country
house architect when he made this little
sketchbook, a whimsical present for his
childhood friend Barbara Webb, who he
affectionately called 'Ba-lamb.' As a pun
on her nickname, Lutyens has placed two
golden rams on either side of the entrance
to her imaginary waterside palace.
Although a fantasy, the domes and
massing foreshadow his design for the
Viceroy's House in New Delhi, India,
more than a decade later. Mrs Webb was
seriously ill at the time of the gift, and
Lutyens' little present poignantly hints at a
heavenly mansion to come.

78.
Edwin Lutyens (1869–1944)
Design for house, Gravesend, Kent for Captain E.W.S. Day, 1919

Captain Day was the master of the ship in which Lutyens sailed upon his return to Britain from a visit to South Africa in 1919. This was the same year that Lutyens designed the Cenotaph in Whitehall. Although the architect of such weighty and mammoth projects as New Delhi, the new capital of India, Lutyens was endlessly making little sketches, illustrating his letters, and scribbling caricatures of friends and those he met on his travels. With little to do on the voyage home, the architect designed this house for Captain Day, who was approaching retirement. Although the full design of the house is lost (if there ever was one), this 'inventory & some inventions' of the contents (of course never seen by Lutyens) is pure whimsy. A model of the house stands behind the Captain and his wife in the final sheet, inscribed '& yet another Day!'.

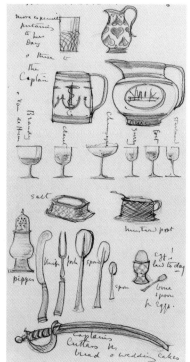

76.
Berthold Lubetkin (1901–90)
Peter Yates, draughtsman
Alternative designs, unexecuted, for prefabricated house fronts, for the 100 House Scheme, Thornhill Gill Housing, Peterlee, County Durham, c. 1949

The ultra-modern architect Berthold Lubetkin produced this set of designs to demonstrate to the planning committee of Peterlee New Town, which he was designing, that different façades could be applied to prefabricated house shells. The array of styles ranges from the traditional to the futuristic, from the capricious to the purposely outright ridiculous. However, hampered by government interference for his overall scheme, Lubetkin not only pulled out of the project, but left architecture altogether to take up pig farming. As one contemporary said, 'Lubetkin had finally met his Peterloo.'

Private Worlds

134.
Clough Williams-Ellis (1883–1978)
Perspective by H.F. Waring
*Capriccio for rebuilding Plas Brondanw,
Merioneth, Wales,* 1913

In the lower-right corner, the architect sits
with his bride-to-be, Annabel Strachey,
admiring the great house he wishes to
build for her. Although the actual small
stone house on the site that they purchased
never grew to such magnificence, the
Williams-Ellis' lived there contentedly for
62 years, creating a beautiful garden. They
were also close to Sir Clough's great fantasy
creation, the village of Portmeirion.

112.
Robert Smythson (*c.* 1535–1614)
*Design for a house in the form of a Greek cross,
c.* 1580s

The celebrated architect of Elizabethan
England, Robert Smythson built such
magnificent country houses as Wollaton
Hall and Worksop Manor, both in
Nottinghamshire, and Hardwick Hall,
Derbyshire. This little plan is for a house
in a distinctive pattern – a quatrefoil is laid
over a square. Where the two shapes meet
are the four staircases, with yet two more
squares for the central court and outer
perimeter wall. The Elizabethans loved
pattern, which they linked to theories on
universal harmony.

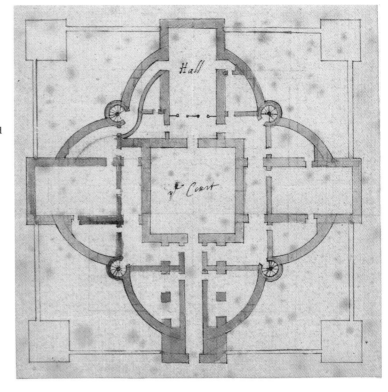

111.
John Smythson, attributed (d. 1634)
Design for a pavilion in a formal landscape,
c. 1620

John Smythson, son of the renowned
architect Robert Smythson, followed
in his father's footsteps, keeping alive
the sixteenth-century love of geometric
pattern. His little pavilion sits in a garden
of criss-crossing paths. The architectural
historian, Sir Howard Colvin, has noted
that Smythson's style was 'mannered
almost to the point of eccentricity, but
unexpectedly attractive as well as whimsical.'

Private Worlds

114.

Softroom (est. 1994)
Floating Retreat, 1997

Commissioned by *Wallpaper** magazine
to design a series of spaces for twenty-first-
century living, Softroom responded with
a number of concepts, from a retractable
home like a Swiss Army Knife to a high-
tech tree house and the private tow-away
desert island complete with its own beach
– created by inflating the contents
of a pod – shown here.

99.
Eric Parry (b. 1952)
Study for Villa of the Physicists, 1985

This competition entry for the design of
a villa to be built as a Lego model, is based
on a structure described in Friedrich
Dürrenmatt's play *The Physicists*. Converted
into a sanatorium, Dürrenmatt's villa is the
backdrop for the investigation into the
murder of a psychiatric nurse. The
suspects are the patients, all deluded
atomic physicists who – 'each rapt in the
cocoon of his own little world' – believe
themselves to be famous scientists such as
Newton and Einstein.

129.

Charles Francis Annesley Voysey
(1857–1941)
*Design for a wallpaper or textile, called
'The Dream', 1889*

The Arts and Crafts architect and designer
C.F.A. Voysey was not fond of his father, the
Reverand Charles Voysey, who had broken
away from the Church of England and
founded a so-called scientific system of
belief he called 'Theism'. Perhaps this is
part of the younger Voysey's reaction, a
vision of hell – a very peculiar but colourful
subject for a wallpaper or textile.

74.

James Kennedy-Hawkes (b. 1913)
*'Sketch design for holiday cottage on the East
Coast', 1941*

This apparently simple drawing is of
heart-aching desire, a little cottage near
the English seaside. It was composed by
the architect Kennedy-Hawkes while a
prisoner of war in a camp near Eichstatt,
Germany. Captured in Crete in 1941,
Kennedy-Hawkes was able to obtain
drawing materials in captivity from the
Germans, he recalled, 'at a price'. He
even taught architectural classes to fellow
internees. After the Second World War,
Kennedy-Hawkes lived and worked quietly
as an architect, retiring to a little brick
cottage in Surrey.

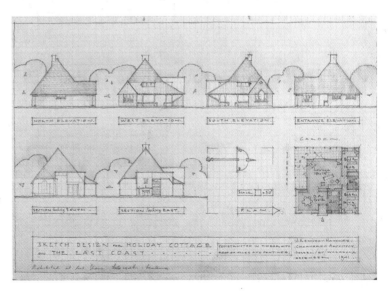

Appliance of Science

92.
NASA Ames Research Center (est. 1939)
Toroidal Colonies, c. 1970s

Having spent the 1960s implementing a
programme to demonstrate the potential
of space travel, during the next decade
NASA commissioned a series of studies
into the feasibility of developing large-scale
human settlements in space. These artistic
renderings of colonies housing up to
10,000 people transpose all-American
suburbia into orbit. Each free-floating
settlement is contained within gigantic
cylinders, spheres and tori. These are
designed to be air-tight so as to hold a
breathable atmosphere and to rotate in
pseudo-gravity. NASA speculated that
space colonies might eventually prove
very attractive for certain sectors of the
population. They also envisaged that
eventually most people in space
settlements would be born there, and
that some day they may vastly exceed
the Earth's population.

Appliance of Science

4.
Alsop Architects (est. 1979)
The Fourth Grace, 2002

This scheme is set to transform the iconic waterfront horizon of Liverpool's Pier Head when it is completed in time for the city's hosting of the European Capital of Culture in 2008. The structure will contain retail, commercial, office, residential and hotel spaces, a 'garden in the sky' overlooking the river, as well as new exhibition areas for the National Museum of Liverpool. It will join the trio of existing historic mercantile buildings, dubbed 'The Three Graces', whose profiles have long dominated the view across the River Mersey. But in contrast to their four-square and pinnacled profiles, this 'fourth grace' will be a voluptuous sculptural 'cloud' created from a combination of three structural solutions, including a diamond-gridded atrium structure which supports the roof.

69.
Ron Herron (1930–1995); Archigram
W.C. 'Moving', 1964

Herron described his *Walking City* as a 'world capital'. Giant 40-storey nomadic urban machines – looking rather like giant dust-mites, with telescopic legs and arms and their own microclimates – were designed to roam in herds across the planet. These could then connect up to each other, where conditions allow, to form a larger metropolis: 'Moscow, a desert, New York Harbor, a Pacific Atoll and the Thames Estuary, any place and every place, a world capital of total probability.' With change, movement and flexibility – or 'indeterminancy' as he described it – the increasingly dominant characteristics of modern urban living, Herron took the logical step of designing a whole city to reflect this condition.

7.
Ove Nyquist Arup (1895–1988)
Sketch designs for Opera House, Sydney, Australia, 1961

In this sketch, Ove Arup plays with shapes
for the famous overlapping shells of
Sydney Opera House. The competition
for the structure had been won in 1957
by the Danish architect, Jørn Utzon; but
frustrated by government interference,
Utzon resigned during construction,
leaving Arup as engineer in charge of
the difficult task of working out how to
design the structural complexities of the
pre-stressed concrete shells, which many
critics thought impossible to build. Arup's
successful completion of the project
resulted in Australia's most famous building.

21.
Eduardo Fernando Catalano (b. 1917)
Drawing to illustrate the structure of warped surfaces and columns, 1952–57

Catalano's studies of hyperbolic
paraboloids were preparations for long-
span roof structures. The Argentinian
architect, who settled in the United States,
in fact built a similar type of warping roof
on his own house in North Carolina.
A theorist as much as an architect, in 1995
Catalano wrote the book *La constante*,
a philosophical dialogue between an
architect and a mathematician discussing
aesthetics, history, geometry, structure
and space.

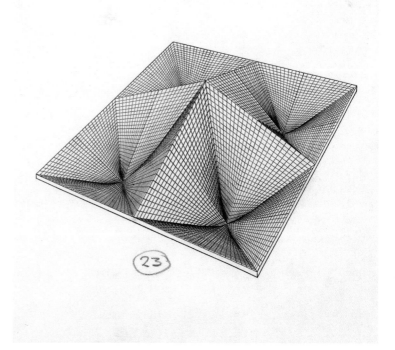

25.
James Clephan (*fl.* 1815–50)
*Design, unexecuted, for an elevated railway,
London, c.* 1845

Two innovations – the pneumatic railway
and massive structural cast iron – are
combined in this scheme for an elevated
transport network for London. Having no
engine, the train appears to be propelled
by air pressure through the tube below.
The guard perches on a small seat outside
the carriages. During the 1840s, railway
mania was at its peak. Pneumatic railways,
also known as atmospheric railways, were
considered a cheap and clean alternative
to steam. A few short lines of no more than
15 miles were built in England and France,
but they all proved to be quick failures.

PERSPECTIVE VIEW OF THE LONDON RAILWAY.

36.
Ronald Aver Duncan (1889–1960)
Design for the 'House of the Future', Ideal
Home *exhibition, Olympia, Hammersmith
and Fulham, London,* 1928

The annual *Ideal Home* exhibition
in London is not usually known for its
cutting-edge design, although the House
of the Future section has produced notable
exceptions. Duncan's design would have
been very avant-garde for Britain in 1928,
when flat roof Modernism of this type had
barely touched UK shores. The unique
drawing style is derived from the Italian
Futurists, with its sharp and whiplash lines.

OLYMPIA
FEB 26. 1928.

29.
Peter Cook (b. 1936)
Design for Solar City, 1980

Peter Cook is well known for blurring the
lines between fantasy and reality. As part
of the Archigram group of the 1960s and
1970s, Cook developed many visionary
projects that, although they were never
realised, soon began to influence the
way we live, especially in terms of their
technological capabilities. *Design for Solar
City* shows a series of solar-panelled houses
arranged in cells, shown as criss-cross
surfaces set around courtyards.

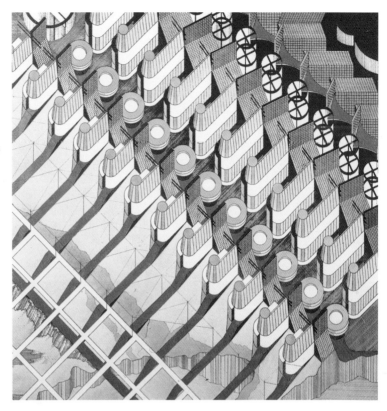

49.
Richard Buckminster Fuller (1895–1983)
*Sketch for a geodesic dome, inscribed 'To Tom /
with affectionate regard / Bucky Fuller Jan 29
1972'*, 1972

A visionary, utopian and at times extremely
practical designer, Buckminster Fuller's
invention of the geodesic dome captured
the imagination of the 1960s generation.
Made of triangular units, a geodesic dome
is strong yet lightweight. In one of his most
famous schemes he pictured a large section
of Manhattan covered by a geodesic dome
(fig.7); he said that 'a fleet of sixteen of the
large Sikorsky helicopters could fly all the
segments into position in three months
at a cost of $200m.' Although this project
was never realised, several of his geodesic
domes were built, like the United States
Pavilion at Expo '67 in Montreal, Canada.

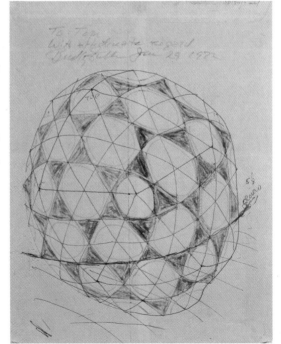

53.
Stephen Geary (1797–1854)
*Design for Cosmos Institute, Leicester Square,
London, c. 1830*

At the centre of this building, which would
have replaced the garden within Leicester
Square, is a global room for a diorama: an
immense painted canvas unfurled around
the walls and specially lit to heighten the
atmospheric impression. The architect-
engineer Stephen Geary holds the honour
of having laid out London's Highgate
Cemetery and designing the city's first
gin palace.

62.
Joseph Hartland (*fl.* 1833)
*'Plan for removing houses. As adopted in the
United States by Letter Patent'*, 1833

This charming and naïve drawing shows
four men effortlessly lifting and rolling
away a Georgian townhouse. Moving
houses about has always been a fairly
common practice in America. It is implied
that this method of house moving is so
simple – although not very explanatory
from this drawing – that the tenant has
not even taken down the curtains in the
windows.

110.
Geoff Shearcroft (b. 1977) / AOC
Grow Your Own, 2001

This 'house on a mouse', inspired by the
notorious experiment to grow a human
ear on the back of a rodent, was originally
exhibited under the spoof headline:
'UK researcher warns of a growth in the
housing market.' This possible solution
to the shortage of new housing stock in
the UK juxtaposes the comforting idea
of a conventional home with a nightmare
scenario of biotechnology gone mad.
As the designer exhorts: 'Our homes will
grow in this brave new world. Our growths
will become home. Why let the experts
design and build, when we have the tools
to evolve 'n' mould. Go forth good citizens
and grow your own.'

75.
William Low (1824–1906)
Design for 'Channel Tunnel Railway', 1868

The first serious ideas for constructing
a foot tunnel connecting England and
France date to the beginning of the
nineteenth century; but fears of Napoleon
and his army invading scuppered any such
plans. The coming of the railway, however,
offered a faster means of transport and
many untested schemes. How to ventilate
the smoke from the steam trains,
as used in this scheme by Low (and not
explained), was always a drawback to
construction. The two points of departure
marked on the map – St Margaret's on the
English side, and Sangatte on the French –
were considered the best places for drilling
through the soft chalk.

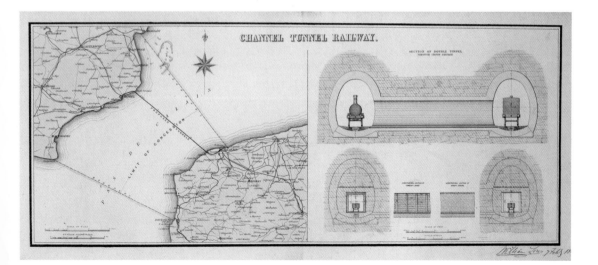

81.
Virgilio Marchi (1895–1960)
'Spatial Study', 1919

This study sums up two principal themes
of the Italian Futurists: movement and the
dynamic quality of the city. Marchi created
a series of similar studies, all based on
conical shapes. Here they intertwine at the
top of a fantasy building, no doubt in
homage to the poem 'Cones' written in
1910 by the Futurist poet Aldo Polazzeschi:

> The highest windows
> underneath the roofs,
> Shaped like cones …
> Cones of the roofs,
> cones of the hands,
> cones of the doors,
> cones of the trees,
> cones of the wings,
> cones, cones.

84.
Raymond McGrath (1903–77)
*Design for British Broadcasting Corporation
dance and chamber music studio, Broadcasting
House, Langham Place, London*, 1929

Fantasy through drawing technique.
The young Modernist Raymond McGrath
presented his design for a studio in the new
BBC building as a densely coloured
axonometric, a projection whereby both
plan and perspective together are
represented to scale. The effect is abstract,
influenced by the painterly qualities of the
Dutch De Stijl movement. McGrath's
studio was built, but has since been destroyed.

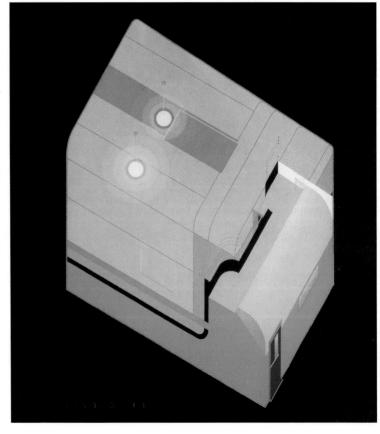

79.
Greg Lynn (b. 1964); FORM
Ark of the World, 2002

Once completed, this building will be
a multidisciplinary museum and cultural
centre for Costa Rica devoted to natural
history, ecology and contemporary art.
Its complexity of form is made possible
through the latest computer-aided
software, which Lynn has described as
enabling architects to stop thinking about
rigid boxes and start thinking about
flexible 'blobs'. Whilst the design is
inspired by the flora and fauna of the
Central American rainforest and its colour
influenced by that of tree frogs there is
more than a nod, as the architect freely
admits, to the mutated 'blobs' of science
fiction B-movies.

94.
Nils Norman (b. 1966)
*Proposed Redevelopment of the Oval, Hackney
E2, London. Renamed: Let the Blood of the
Private Property Developers Run Freely in the
Streets of Hackney, Playscape Complex A.*, 2003

For the past decade the artist Nils Norman
has been devising imaginative proposals
for community-based initiatives to
improve urban living conditions.
Conscious that blind devotion to social
progress under Modernism has often been
misguided and destructive, Norman's
projects habitually strike a careful balance
between parodying visionary zeal and
maintaining faith in alternative solutions
to contemporary civic malaise. This
scheme converts a cluster of light industrial
buildings, two crescents of slum terraces
and a makeshift car park in the heart of
East London, into a self-sustainable
enclave. The development comprises a
small wetland to increase local bio-diversity
(created by redirecting the nearby canal);
an adventure playground with a
labyrinthine network of walkways, ladders,
catwalks, swings and platforms, an
educational facility and an indoor Info-
Park with production and printing centres
focusing on anti-capitalist and anti-
corporate strategies and issues.

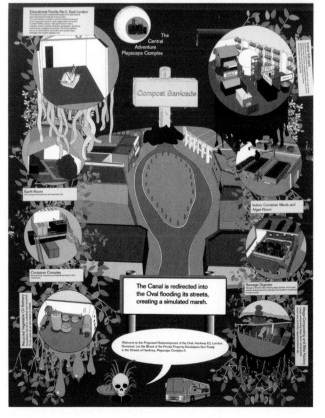

48.
Freedom Ship International Inc.
Freedom Ship, 2002 (detail)

Once completed, *Freedom Ship* will be 4,500
feet long and 750 feet wide; more than four
times larger than the Queen Mary. Too slow
to be a cruise or cargo ship, this immense
steel barge will move slowly around the
world, hugging the shoreline and
completing one revolution every three
years. The vessel's superstructure, rising 25
stories above its broad main deck, will
house residential space, a library, schools
and a hospital in addition to a vast duty-free
shopping mall, banks, hotels, restaurants,
casinos, athletic facilities, offices,
warehouses and light manufacturing and
assembly enterprises. The ship's top deck
will serve private and small commercial
aircraft which will ferry residents and
visitors to and from shore.

28.
Peter Cook (b. 1936); Archigram
Plug-In City; Max. pressure area, 1964

The most innovative of the so-called 'radical' architectural groups of the 1960s, Archigram (a combination of the words 'architecture' and 'telegram') invented new artefacts and situations that threatened the discipline of architecture itself. Like many of the group's inventions, *Plug-In City* first appeared in *Archigram*, the magazine that the group published between 1961 and 1974, where it was described as 'a large-scale network-structure, containing access ways and essential services which can be applied to any terrain'. Into this network were placed units that were planned for obsolescence: bathrooms to last three years; house units 15 years; car silos and roads 20 years; the main megastructure 40 years. The units were to be served and manoeuvred by means of cranes operating from a railway at the apex of the structure and the interior contained 'electronic and machine installations intended to replace present-day work operations.' Archigram envisaged that a network of *Plug-In Cities* would eventually link all the existing centres of population in Great Britain, making a 'total city'.

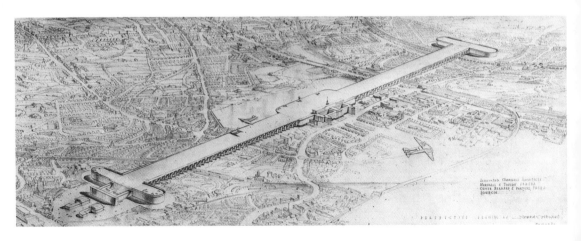

10.
John Belcher (1841–1913)
Perspective by William Bingham
McGuiness
*Competition design, unexecuted, for the South
Kensington Museum, now the Victoria and
Albert Museum, London, 1891*

John Belcher was a respected late-
Victorian architect of commercial and
institutional buildings. Like most
architects, when he required drawings for
special occasions – such as to include in
an exhibition, seduce a client or, as in this
case, in the hope of winning a competition
– he hired perspective artists skilled at
presentation. McGuiness, by bending the
rules of perspective and exaggerating the
vaulted spaces, has lifted Belcher's design
to monumental proportions reminiscent
of eighteenth-century stage set designs.

82. (opposite)
Marshall & Tweedy, with Oliver Bernard
and Partners
Aerial perspective by Norman Howard
*Design, unexecuted, for Hendon airport,
London, c. 1935*

London's first airport – a traditional,
stripped Neo-Classical looking brick
station at Croydon – opened in 1920.
By the 1930s, it was stylistically outdated
and many architects, on speculation,
created visionary schemes reflecting the
excitement of modern air travel. Here,
futuristic aeroplanes circle over an
enormous elevated landing strip which
incorporates the terminal building and
hangars. The eventual site of London's
new airport at Heathrow was not chosen
until 1943.

Megastructures

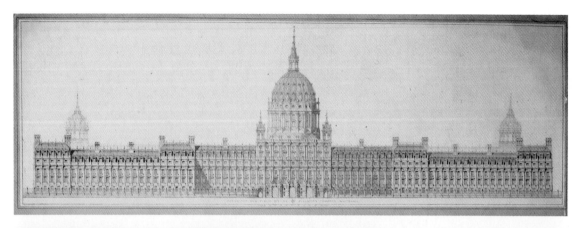

9. (top)
Charles Barry (1795–1860)
*Design for a Palace of Government Offices,
Whitehall, London,* 1858 (detail)

Having sorted out the politicians with his
Houses of Parliament, Barry turned his
attention at the end of his career to a
solution for centralising the civil service
in a great palace of bureaucracy.
A competition held in 1857 for new
government offices in Whitehall had led
to controversy over style and planning.
Barry responded with this grand gesture,
which was much admired for its bravura,
a visionary dream on a scale too imperially
costly even for Imperial Britain.

14. (bottom)
Etienne-Louis Boullée (1728–99)
Design for a Metropolitan Cathedral, 1782

Boullée is the ultimate of visionary
architects, and this is one of his most
famous pen drawings. In this mighty
cathedral, the vanishing point along
tunnels of columns and vaulted ceilings
terminates in clouds of incense rising
from around the altar during High
Mass. Boullée envisioned the building
dominating Paris from the heights of
Montmartre or Mont Valérien.

101.
Joseph Paxton (1803–65)
The Great Victorian Way, Sydenham, London,
1855

Ten miles long, this covered arcade was
to snake in a ring through and around
London. Joseph Paxton was the innovative
designer of the Crystal Palace, London,
built in 1851, and had co-ordinated the
exhibition building's dismantling and
re-erection in Sydenham a few years later.
His *Great Victorian Way* was to have been of
the same dimensions and also constructed
of glass and brightly painted iron. In some
sections, as shown here, there would be
shops and hotels. And, on the outside,
an elevated railway would run, to be used
by passengers during the day and for
merchandise and coal at night.

103.
Giovanni Battista Piranesi (1720–78)
Imaginary Prison, plate XIV, 2nd edition, 1761

Piranesi's engravings from the *Carceri
d'Invenzione (Imaginary Prisons)* series are
amongst the greatest of all architectural
fantasies. Shadowy figures haunt the
cavernous worlds of staircases, massive
stone arches, timbered beams, scaffolding,
winches, pulleys and ropes. The
architecture of ancient Rome, which
Piranesi studied and engraved in haunting
detail, has been imaginatively manipulated
as settings of nightmares and persecution.
These dark and haunting images have held
a powerful influence over many later
architects, artists and set designers.

Megastructures

27.
Constant (Constant A. Nieuwenhuys)
(b. 1920)
View of New Babylonian Sectors, 1971

New Babylon is based on the premise that society in the future will be totally automated with the need to work replaced with a nomadic life of creative play. This single piece of architecture, eventually propagating to cover the entire planet, consists of a labyrinthine network of enormous multi-storey interior spaces, through which its inhabitants wander on foot. The interconnected 'sectors' float above the ground on tall columns, with vehicles rushing underneath and air traffic using the roof to land. For Constant, a Dutch artist, *New Babylon* was both a realisable project and also a form of propaganda critiquing conventional social structures. Believing that the traditional arts would be replaced by a collective form of creativity, he saw it as heralding the end of the distinction between art and architecture, and it has had a major influence on the work of subsequent generations of architects. This image belongs to an extensive series of models, sketches, etchings, lithographs, architectural drawings and photocollages, as well as manifestos, essays, lectures and films that he produced between 1957 and 1974 relating to this project.

70.
Charles Holden (1875–1960)
Perspective by A. Bryett
*Design, known as 'Spiral Scheme II',
partially executed, for the University
of London, Bloomsbury, London,* 1933

By the 1930s, the University of London,
with an ever-widening network of
colleges spread across the city, required
a central administration building
and library. Purchasing a ten-and-a-half
acre site to the north of the British
Museum, the university commissioned
Charles Holden as their architect. Holden's
vision was monolithic. Financial restraint,
that bugbear of many a great vision, meant
only the southern end, which came to be
called Senate House, was built.

83.
Leslie Martin (1908–2000)
*Design for a National and Government Centre,
Whitehall, London,* 1965

In the 1960s, with Modernism at its peak
and the appreciation of Georgian and
Victorian architecture at its nadir, Sir
Leslie Martin's massive government office
building in Whitehall would have wiped
away the historic administrative heart of
Great Britain. In terms of town planning,
the concept was controlled and, at a
maximum of seven stories, the building
did not compete with the towers of
Westminster. Martin, respected for his
conception of the Royal Festival Hall on
London's South Bank, was an influential
teacher who based his design solutions
on 'the grid as generator', which is clearly
seen in this scheme. The stepped-back
form of the structure, however, was
dubbed by the *Architects' Journal* as
'ziggurats for bureaucrats'.

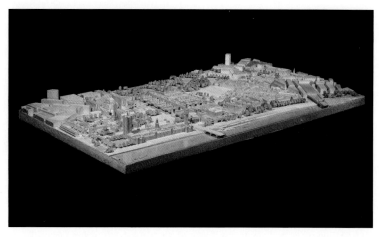

Megastructures

8.
Asymptote (est. 1989): Hani Rashid
and Lisa Anne Couture
New York Virtual Stock Exchange, 1997–2000

Designed as 'a dynamic, fluctuating world
of data' this virtual environment allows
stockbrokers to navigate through
continuously updated trading information
on the stock exchange in real time and in
three dimensions. Wall Street has always
been at the cutting edge of information
technology, installing telephones on the
trading floor in 1878, but this visualisation
of the relentless workings of global
capitalism as a vast structural landscape
was inspired by the swarming vistas of
heaven and hell seen in Hieronymous
Bosch's fifteenth-century painting,
The Garden of Earthly Delights (fig.12).

121.
Superstudio (est. 1966)
The Continuous Monument – New New York,
1969

This seemingly endless structure, whose
white-gridded framework extends across
the entire surface of the earth – literally
a global megastructure – was a critique
of contemporary urban planning and the
deadening strictures of Modernism. As
Adolfo Natalini, one of the five architects
who founded Superstudio in Florence
in 1966, explains, '...in 1969, we started
designing negative utopias like *The
Continuous Monument* – images warning
of the horrors architecture had in store
with its scientific methods for perpetuating
standard models worldwide. Of course,
we were also having fun.' This print is one
of a series taken from photomontages that
show this structure in radically different
situations – crossing the Alps, wrapping
around the Taj Mahal and here stretching
across midtown Manhattan.

45.
Foreign Office Architects (est. 1992)
The Bundle Tower, 2002

This proposal, originally developed as a
design for a competition organised by the
Max Protech Gallery in New York, replaces
Minoru Yamasaki's Twin Towers with six
sinuous structures, like a bunch of
filaments under the microscope. Braced
by an external steel lattice, these multiple
towers interconnect every 36 floors,
buttressing each other and sharing floor
space for maximum flexibility. The series
of interconnections allow the towers to
share the 12 high-speed lifts and two
stairwells contained in each, thus
providing a very effective fire escape
system. Whilst safer than the original
buildings, this scheme is also taller,
re-establishing and echoing the original
structure of the World Trade Center as
an important landmark at the tip of
Manhattan Island.

17.
W. Bridges (*fl.* 1793)
*'A plan and elevation for a bridge over the River
Avon at the Rocks of St Vincent from Sion Row,
Clifton to Leigh Down near Bristol Hot Well',*
1793

This multi-storied bridge was to have been
wedged into the Clifton Gorge at Bristol.
Above its single arch span, the structure
incorporated a chapel, public offices,
warehouses and a corn exchange. Of the
architect and the circumstances of the
scheme, nothing is known; Isambard
Kingdom Brunel's suspension bridge,
designed in 1829, is its famous successor.

131.
Alfred Waterhouse (1830–1905)
*Competition design for the Royal Courts
of Justice, Strand, London*, 1866 (detail)

The great Victorian architect of such
buildings as the Natural History Museum
dreams here of a new Gothic London
which, he said, could be 'picturesque
of external form with the most rigid
utilitarianism.' This perspective is by
Waterhouse himself.

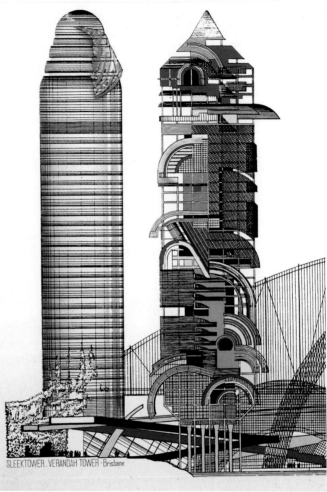

SLEEKTOWER . VERANDAH TOWER - Brisbane

19.
Stefan Buzas (b. 1915)
*Competition design, unexecuted, for the
'Vertical Feature', 1951 Festival of Britain,
South Bank, London, c. 1950*

The Festival of Britain in 1951 celebrated
the optimism of a country emerging from
the ashes of the Second World War. The
main festival site was on the South Bank,
London, with exhibition and fairground
buildings designed in the new Modern
style. Its beacon was a tower, for which a
competition was held to find a design. Stefan
Buzas, a Hungarian immigrant architect,
submitted this drawing for a steel frame
structure hung with colourful banners,
incorporating a viewing platform and an
aerial for bouncing signals off the moon
(a competition requirement). The winning
design, a suspended space needle, the Skylon,
was by the architects Powell and Moya.

30.
Peter Cook (b.1936)
*Design for Sleektower and Verandah Tower,
Brisbane, Queensland, Australia, 1984*

When visiting Brisbane on a teaching
assignment, Peter Cook came up with this
imaginative design for a pair of contrasting
high-rise buildings to give the city skyline
greater impact. Like a large plastic water
bottle, *Sleektower* is in the mould of
International Style skyscrapers; while
its colourful companion is hung with
verandas, a feature the architect admired
on many of the old local houses.

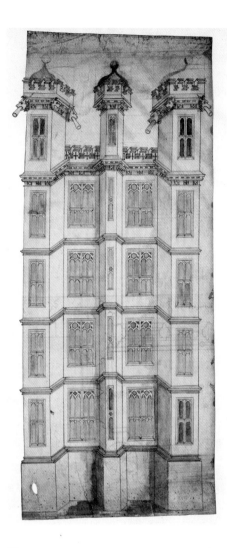

40.
English (late-fifteenth or early-sixteenth-century master)
Design for a tower with turrets, c. 1490–1510

This design appears to have been intended for a royal palace or grand country house of the Tudor period. Topped by crenellated towers with arrow loops, the fortified appearance of the tower is merely a style of romantic chivalry. The Tudor court enjoyed the pageantry and trappings of the earlier medieval period, which extended into their architecture. But for all its castle-like qualities, such elements as the large windows would have proved useless in any real battle.

46.
Foster and Partners (est. 1967)
M Tower, Tokyo, 1993

At 840 metres high, this 170 storey tower, commissioned by the Obayashi Corporation, might have been the world's tallest building had its construction not been impeded by a massive economic downturn in the Far East. Proposed as a solution to the continuing expansion of Tokyo, it was to be sited two kilometres offshore in Tokyo Bay. Designed to house 60,000 people, the structure also provides spaces for work and leisure with light manufacturing industries, department stores and apartments. Topped by wind and solar generators that provide for all its energy needs, and with a high-speed 'metro' system, tracking both horizontally and vertically, it was to have been a virtually self-sufficient vertical city quarter.

89.
MVRDV (est. 1991)
Pig City, 2001

This design provides a logical solution
to the clash between urbanisation and
farming in Europe's most densely
populated country and chief exporter
of pork. In 1999 The Netherlands was
officially inhabited by 15.2 million pigs
and 15.5 million humans. Just as the
Dutch have reclaimed land from the sea
for horizontal agricultural development
this project investigates ways to create
space vertically. *Pig City* references earlier
visionary schemes such as Frank Lloyd
Wright's 1958 Broadacre City and
Le Corbusier's 1935 Ville Radieuse
(an unrealised scheme to flatten the
overcrowded historic centre of Paris to
make way for a high-rise utopia). To limit
the risk of disease spreading, each tower
in *Pig City* is self-sufficient with a
slaughterhouse located at ground level
and 40 pig farms stacked above. The
structures are located along the coastline
in artificially flooded land used to breed
tilapia fish that in turn provide a protein
supply for the livestock. The domes at the
summit of each tower collect methane
from the pig's manure, which in turn
generates the necessary power to service
the city.

107.
Thomas Rickman (1776–1841)
and Richard Charles Hussey (1802–87)
*Competition design for the Fitzwilliam Museum,
Cambridge*, 1834

A museum as gothic cathedral. In
academic cap and gown, Cambridge staff
and students gather beneath Rickman
and Hussey's design for a great tower,
which was for effect only as it housed
neither museum objects nor accommodation.
The picturesque qualities of the building's
design owed much to James Wyatt's
Fonthill Abbey, Wiltshire, where the
fantastic 300 foot tower had collapsed
in 1825. The competition for the
Fitzwilliam Museum was won by George
Basevi, whose design was in a Classical style.

109.
R. Seifert (1910–2001) and Partners
Perspective by A.F. Gill
*Design for an office building, Melbourne,
Australia, c. 1970*

It is alleged that Colonel Richard Seifert
has been responsible for more buildings
in Great Britain than any other architect.
His much-admired Centre Point at St Giles'
Circus, London, has been called Britain's
first Pop skyscraper. Seifert's empire
extended across Africa and, as we can see
here, as far as Australia, although this great
tower, with its swooping base, was not built.
A.F. Gill was Seifert's favourite perspective
artist, able to lift the often commercially
banal into a glossy package.

120.
Paolo Soleri (b. 1919)
Design for an arcology, 1977

The visionary architect Paolo Soleri lives
and works in the utopian desert
community of Arcosanti, Arizona, which
he began to create in 1970. It is his model
'arcology', a harmonious marriage of
architecture and ecology. Less than ten per
cent finished, the New-Age project is self-
funded mainly through the sale of wind
chimes. Soleri has proposed many types
of arcologies, most on an enormous scale,
with megastructures for up to six-million
inhabitants. This one is modest, an
arcology city housed in twin towers.

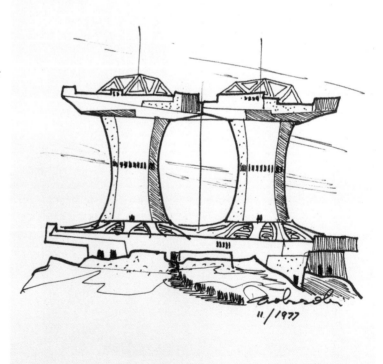

125.
Philip Armstrong Tilden (1887–1956)
*Design for a tower for Selfridges department
store, Oxford Street, London*, 1918

The department store owner Gordon
Selfridge kept the architect Philip Tilden
in his employ. As such, Tilden was required
to create designs continually for Selfridge,
including a large unbuilt castle. Some of
Tilden's schemes were practical; some,
like this proposal for Selfridge's Oxford
Street store, were simply masterful fantasy
drawings. The design of the tower is based
loosely on the ancient Mausoleum at
Halicarnassus, and one wonders if Tilden
is suggesting to Selfridge that he might
make his tomb over the shop.

128.
King Vidor (1894–1982)
The Fountainhead, 1949 (still)

Adapted by novelist and screenwriter
Ayn Rand from her best-selling novel,
The Fountainhead focuses on the
uncompromising philosophical stance
of its protagonist, Howard Roark – played
here by Gary Cooper. In defence of artistic
integrity and individualism Roark blows-up
a partially-constructed building site called
Cortland Homes because it has been
altered from his original design to conform
to public taste. The sparse Modernism of
Roark's designs, meticulously created for
the film, is based closely on the work of
Frank Lloyd Wright (1869–1959), perhaps
the greatest American architect of the
twentieth century. Lloyd Wright was a
student of another pioneering American
Modernist, Louis Sullivan (1856–1924),
and the parallels between the two men and
their fictional counterparts – Roark and his
mentor Henry Cameron – are unavoidable.
In this scene Roark's clients suggest adding
Classical details to soften the harsh
Modern lines of his design for a skyscraper.

133.
Wim Wenders (b. 1945)
Until the End of the World, 1991 (still)
'Endless Tower' designed by Jean Nouvel
(b.1945)

The plot of this ambitious production
set in the year 1999 revolves around the
invention of a device that enables the
viewer to send images directly to the brain.
The conception and operation of this
device is in stark contrast to a deteriorating
global situation, where the continued
existence of humanity is under threat from
a nuclear powered satellite falling towards
earth. In this scene, computer simulation
is used to create a view of La Défense, the
vast business district on the outskirts of
Paris which, at the time the film was made,
was in the relatively early stages of
construction. Here we see the completed
Grande Arche and Jean Nouvel's *Tour Sans
Fin (Endless Tower)*, a major and, to date,
unrealised project for an office building
that rises dramatically into the sky to
disappear visually into the clouds in a haze
of coloured, transparent glass. Nouvel's
architecture is heavily informed by cinema
and contingent ideas about light and
transparency: one of his early projects for a
nightclub literally recreates a scene from
Wender's *Der Stand der Dinger (The State of
Things)*, 1982.

38.
Elgo Plastics Inc., Chicago, Illinois, USA
American Skyline, first manufactured 1956

With *American Skyline*, budding architects
could build to scale (using HO, the model
railway scale), a rarity in building sets. The
instruction booklet displays a plastic city
of skyscrapers made of interlocking
components, duplicating in a simplified
manner actual building construction
methods. The set, made of plastic,
emphasises to the child that cities can
be clean, white, of new materials and,
above all, modern.

18.
David Butler (1894–1979)
Just Imagine, 1930 (still) (detail)

The first science fiction musical ever made,
Just Imagine was produced at vast expense
at the height of the Depression: its
futuristic city, purportedly New York in
1980, was constructed in an aircraft hangar
outside Hollywood at a reputed cost of
a quarter of a million dollars. Art director
Stephen Goosson and mechanical effects
director Ralph Hammeras drew
inspiration from the visionary drawings
of the Italian Futurist Antonio Sant'Elia,
and from the work of the architectural
delineator Hugh Ferriss, whose book,
Metropolis of Tomorrow (fig.2), published the
same year as the model's design, reiterated
his vision of widely spaced towers rising
from lower buildings, all linked by
multilevel walkways and bridges.

Urban Futures

63.
Hayes Davidson (est. 1989)
Fast Forward, 2001

In this short film devised to test visual
memory of the urban environment,
advanced computer graphics are
combined with filmed panoramas of
London. New buildings are added to the
skyline and existing buildings are moved
or removed. The result tests the viewer's
ability to recognise change to the city,
and questions how robust, or not, visual
memory of the 'cherished' skyline actually is.

6.
Michael Anderson (b. 1920)
1984, 1956 (still)

In George Orwell's haunting dystopic
novel of 1949, his description of London
as 'chief city of Airstrip One, the most
populous province of Oceania' is clearly
inspired by the devastated cityscape of
post-Blitz London with its 'vistas of rotting
nineteenth-century houses [...] and
bombed sites where the plaster dust swirled
in the air and the willow herb straggled
over the heaps of rubble.' This Anglo-
American production made amid the
ruins left by wartime bombing used
models and process photography to create
Orwell's ministries of Peace, Love, Plenty
and Truth – the hive-shaped buildings
seen in this aerial vista. For Orwell,
these sinister edifices are the material
embodiment of Big Brother's totalitarian
regime: 'enormous pyramidal structures
of glittering white concrete, soaring
up, terrace after terrace, three hundred
metres into the air.'

106.
Gason Quiribet
The Fugitive Futurist: A Q-riosity by 'Q',
1924 (still)

In this silent comedy an inventor, who later
turns out to be an escaped lunatic, claims
to have a camera that looks into the future
and shows what several well-known
London landmarks will look like in years
to come. This still shows a solution for
traffic congestion which involves draining
the River Thames.

39.
Maurice Elvey (1887–1967)
High Treason, 1928 (still)

One of the earliest movies with sound
made in the UK, *High Treason* was a
considerable success in its day when it
was seen as an English counterpart to
Fritz Lang's seminal *Metropolis.* Set in
1940 it envisages a tense political situation
between a United Europe – of which
England is part thanks to a fully operational
Channel tunnel – and a United America.
The set design, influenced more by the real
urban landscapes of contemporary lower
Manhattan than by Lang's Expressionist
conception, envisages London as a
congested concrete jungle with skyscrapers
dwarfing St Paul's Cathedral. At the time
the film was made Chicago and New York
were the only skyscraper cities in the world.

37.
EA Games (est. 1989)
SimCity™ originally designed by Will
Wright at Maxis, 1989
SimCity™ *4*, 2003

A computer 'simulation game', *SimCity*™
gives the player the opportunity to
orchestrate the building and development
of a city. Depending on the choices and
design skills of the player, Simulated
Citizens (Sims) move in and build homes,
hospitals, churches, shops and factories,
or move out in search of a better life
elsewhere. As the game's designer Will
Wright explains, *SimCity*™ 'evolved from
another game, *Raid of Bungling Bay*, where
the basic premise was that you flew around
and bombed islands. The game included
an island generator, and I noticed after a
while that I was having more fun building
islands than blowing them up. About the
same time, I also came across the work
of Jay Forrester, one of the first people to
ever model a city on a computer for social
science purposes. Using his theories
I adapted and expanded the *Bungling
Bay* island generator, and *SimCity*™ was
developed from there'. Hugely successful
since its original release in 1987, *SimCity*™
has spawned numerous bootlegs,
imitations and spin-offs including *SimTown*,
SimIsle, *SimFarm* and *SimEarth*, as well as
sequels with ever more elaborate graphic
schemes – *SimCity*™ *4* shown here is the latest.

80.
Virgilio Marchi (1895–1960)
View of a central perimeter road, 1919

Marchi was a member of the Futurist
movement, which developed in Italy in
1909 and aimed to replace aesthetic values
in the arts and architecture with those
of the machine. Although a stage and set
designer for the early cinema, Marchi
wrote two books on Futurist architecture.
In this drawing, he develops the theoretical
city designs by the Futurist architect
Antonio Sant'Elia, who had proclaimed the
beauty of speed, noise, machines and even
pollution. Marchi's tiered buildings radiate
from a wide and raised central boulevard
edged by giant pylons.

34.
Balkrishna V. Doshi (b. 1927)
*'Concept' design for Vidhyadhar Nagar, Jaipur,
Rajasthan, India*, 1980

Doshi is considered India's leading
architect and urban planner. This
colourful silkscreen print is his method
of presenting a study for a new suburban
town founded upon a time-honoured
method of Indian planning. Based on
a three by three grid plan of the early
eighteenth-century planned city of Jaipur,
Doshi believes that his scheme avoids the
failures of the Modernist approach, which
tended to ignore local traditions.

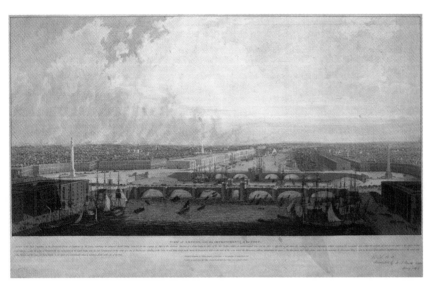

33. (top)
George Dance junior (1741–1825)
'View of London, with the Improvements', 1802

72. (bottom)
Helmut Jacoby (b. 1926)
Town Park, Water Carpet and Cone Area, 1976

From 1796 onwards, George Dance junior, architect for the City of London, presented a series of audacious and magnificent designs for new docks and warehouses along the Thames, while at the same time replacing the old London Bridge a little up-river. The landscape artist William Daniell painted then engraved these suggestions, which proved much too expensive to build. Dance's new bridge is a double crossing, each with a drawbridge; this would have allowed for uninterrupted road passage when a ship passed through.

These central features for a park in Milton Keynes, the UK's last and largest New Town, were never built. Whilst this is a visualisation of a cloudless future for the town's prospective citizens, the proposal – more construction than landscape – simultaneously references the past. Echoing both British sites such as Silbury Hill and pre-Aztec remains in Mexico, it looks almost like the centre for a cult, a feeling underlined in the almost hallucinatory nature of Helmut Jacoby's drawing technique. Before the advent of the computer Jacoby, acknowledged as the world's leading architectural renderer, was renowned for his ability to give life to the ideas that architects reflect in plans, sections and elevations.

86.
Eric Mendelsohn (1887–1953)
Design for White City, Kensington and Chelsea, London, c. 1935

As one of Germany's leading Modern architects, Eric Mendelsohn fled from Nazi persecution to live in England in 1933 before finally settling in the USA in the early 1940s. His scheme for White City in west London was an unrealised design for what would have been one of Europe's largest housing estates. Mendelsohn's drawing is typical of his Expressionist style: rapid and spare, the pencil crayon flicking across the sheet, a great vision reduced to its essentials of vertical and horizontal.

87.
William Cameron Menzies (1896–1957)
Things to Come, 1936 (still)

Adapted from H.G. Wells' science fiction novel of 1933, *The Shape of Things to Come*, this film concerns the collapse and development of civilisation over a hundred-year period. The film begins by introducing us to 'Everytown', then modern London, as it prepares for war on Christmas Eve, 1940. In this scene, we see Everytown in 2036, built in a hollowed-out mountain near the ruins of the old Everytown. The representation of this fabulous new utopia proved a particular challenge to the film's producers and caused them to exceed their budget twice over. The artist Fernand Léger and the architect Le Corbusier were both approached for the role of set designer but declined. It was eventually taken on by artist and inventor László Moholy-Nagy, then briefly resident in London having fled Nazi persecution. Moholy-Nagy went on to head the New Bauhaus in Chicago (1937–39). The designs seen here clearly show the influence of the Russian Constructivist movement with which he is closely associated.

60.
Zaha Hadid (b. 1950)
The Peak Club, Hong Kong, 1982–83

This competition entry for a project for
a leisure club occupies a site on Victoria
Peak, a vantage point overlooking the
world's busiest deepwater port and a
teeming city with a population of nearly
seven million inhabitants. To accentuate
the already dramatic visual conditions of
the site, Hadid inserts elements that impact
vertically and horizontally, 'like knives
cutting though the site'. Hard granite
excavated to level the site is polished and
incorporated into the buildings. The
complex combines facilities that provide
relaxation and respite from Hong Kong's
urban hustle and also a setting for
hedonistic pursuits: swimming pools,
exercise platforms, squash courts, saunas,
restaurants and bars. This project brought
Iraqi-born Hadid international acclaim, not
least for its innovative form of presentation
through the series of gouache paintings
influenced by Russian Suprematism, to
which this work belongs. An influential
teacher and theoretician, Hadid's practice
extends from urban scale designs through
to products, interiors and furniture as well
as stage set and exhibition design.

88.
William Noel Moffett (1912–94)
*Design for redevelopment of Piccadilly Circus,
London*, 1959

Piccadilly Circus has disappeared
completely in this scheme, and the
sculpture of Eros has been raised high
onto a platform in the midst of a shopping
mall. Noel Moffett, who taught at the
Architectural Association, London,
presented this redevelopment on behalf
of 37 schools of architecture, an indication
that most teachers and students of the
period were moonstruck by Modernism.

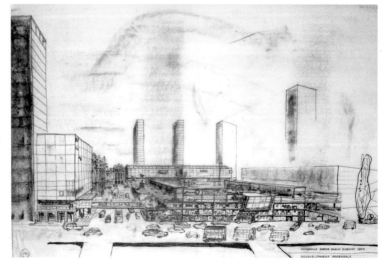

102.
Stephen Rowland Pierce (1896–1966)
*Design for a post-war reconstruction of the
'Metropolis of Britain',* 1942

The air-raid attacks during the Blitz by the
German Luftwaffe from September 1940
to May 1941 left great areas of London and
the industrial cities of Britain in ruin.
Rowland Pierce, the architect of noted Art
Deco town halls at Norwich, Norfolk and
Hammersmith, London, responded with
this suggestion for reconstruction. The
buildings are illustrated in a schematic
form, their outlines suggested only. This
uniformity, understood by a nation at war
used to military direction, makes the
future reassuringly ordered.

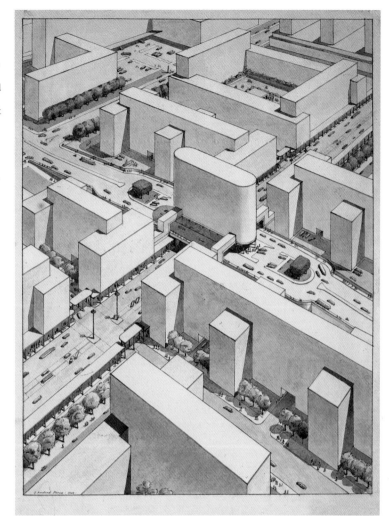

98.
John Buonarotti Papworth (1775–1847)
*Design, unexecuted, for Hygeia, Kentucky,
USA,* 1827

The London-based architect J.B. Papworth,
who never set foot in America, was
commissioned by William Bullock to
design an ideal town on the banks of the
Ohio River opposite Cincinnati. Bullock
was a colourful figure who owned the
Egyptian Hall museum in Piccadilly,
London, a popular art gallery and palace
of varieties behind a Neo-Egyptian temple
façade. The town's name derived from
Hygeia, the Greek goddess of Health.
Papworth's radial scheme differs from the
usual American town planning formula
of the grid system. However, like many other
get-rich-quick land speculations in America,
Bullock's proposal was never realised.

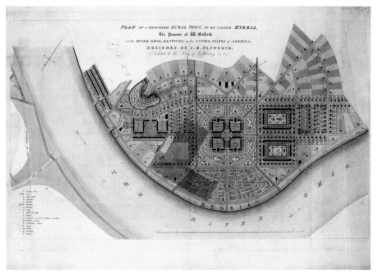

Urban Futures

13.
Birds Portchmouth Russum Architects
(est. 1989)
Croydon, The Future, 1993

Croydon is a business and shopping Mecca
for south-east England but it has an image
problem: its biggest landmark buildings
are car parks which service the thousands
of commuters and shoppers. This scheme
turns a problem into an opportunity, with
the ring of car parks transformed into
fantastical structures that are destinations
in their own right: an arena for archery,
bowls and cricket; a swimming pool;
a concert hall and a skating rink and ski-
slope. These are all connected by a public
tram system to ease traffic problems.
A feasibility study for the scheme to prove
the technical and financial viability of it
was completed but a change in local
government brought the project to a halt.

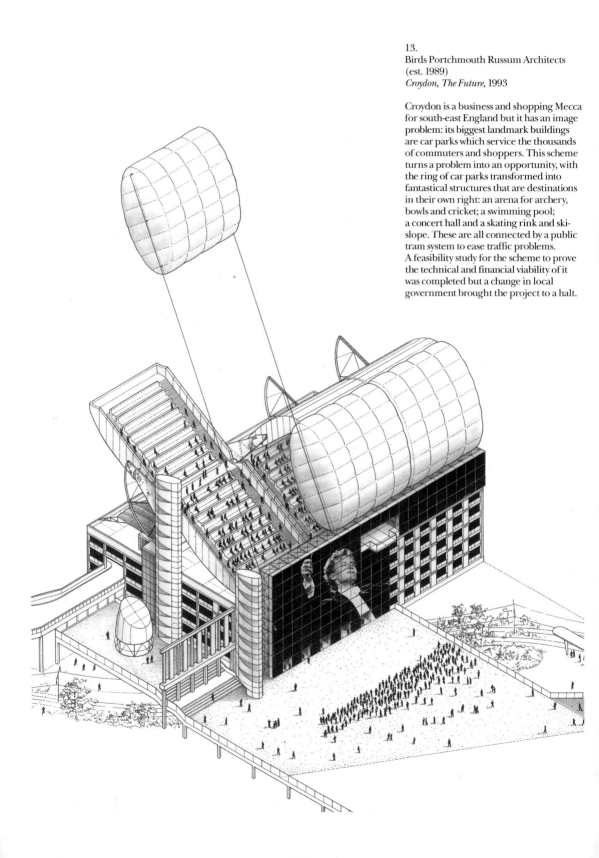

124.
Rodney Thomas (1902–96)
Design for Sky City, c. 1965

Thomas developed *Sky City* as a result of his
study of mass-produced housing after the
Second World War. Machine-made, the
city was to grow like a plant or tree;
Thomas likened it to a lupin receiving the
sun on all its parts. The components of an
everyday city – flats, shops, gardens –
spiral in the sunshine like an earth-based
space station.

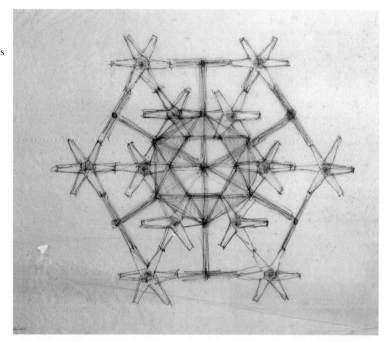

135.
Clough Williams-Ellis (1883–1978)
*Preliminary plan and (insert) elevation
for Melcomb Satellite Town,* 1945

The New Town movement was created
in response to the need to re-house people
who had lost their homes during the
bombings of the Second World War and
to cater to the needs of a growing
population. Although about 28 New Towns
were built – such as Harlow, East Kilbridge
and Milton Keynes – there were plans for
up to 100 in total. Today, the success of
these towns is questioned: were they but
failed utopias? Williams-Ellis' design for
Melcomb is similar in pattern to the star
formation of Renaissance fortress cities.
A high-rise commercial and community
centre is at the heart of radiating
hexagonal housing cells. Not only was the
town not built, but even its intended
location is unclear.

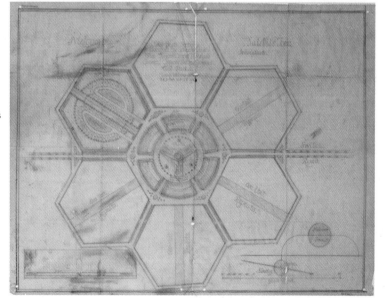

32.
Paul Wegener (1874–1948)
and Carl Boese (1887–1958)
The Golem, 1920, (still)

The Hebrew legend of the Golem has
undergone numerous retellings in the
cinema but this remains the essential
version of the sixteenth-century tale.
The story tells of Rabbi Loew, an alchemist
who prophesises that the Jewish people
are soon to suffer persecution and
responds by sculpting a man of clay (the
Golem) to act as their defender. Made the
same year as Robert Wiene's *The Cabinet of
Doctor Caligari*, *The Golem* does not share
the painted shadows and angular distortion
characteristic of early German
Expressionist cinema. Instead, Wegener
opts for a more subtle stylisation, seen here
in the towering pitched rooftops of the
Prague ghetto. In a lecture of 1916,
Wegener explained, 'everything [in
cinema] depends on image, on a
vagueness of outline where the fantastic
world of the past meets the world of today.'

16.
Henry William Brewer (1836–1903)
Panorama of 'London in the time of Henry VIII', 1887

For 25 years, Brewer was the leading architectural illustrator for *The Builder*, the premier British building magazine of the nineteenth century which published this detailed reconstruction of London in the early sixteenth century. Based upon the latest archaeological and historical information for the period, the view looks west, across the City, with the Tower of London, old St Paul's Cathedral and a crowded London Bridge.

15.
Harold Carlton Bradshaw (1893–1943)
'The Temple of Fortune and its surroundings restored', Palestrina (ancient Praeneste), Italy, 1919

In the footsteps of Andrea Palladio, the young architect H.C. Bradshaw also undertook a great paper restoration of the ancient temple complex at Praeneste. However, unlike Palladio, Bradshaw had the benefit of several centuries of archaeological surveys. Nevertheless, this careful drawing still relies as much upon the architect's imagination as the ruins themselves.

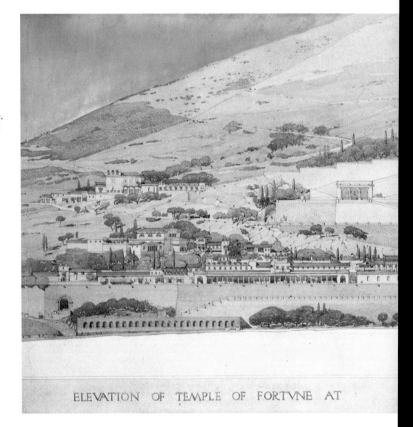

ELEVATION OF TEMPLE OF FORTVNE AT

LONDON
IN THE TIME OF HENRY
H. W. BREWER 1890

AENESTE   AND ITS SVRROVNDINGS RESTORED

Past Perfect

26.
Charles Robert Cockerell (1788–1863)
*Preliminary design for 'The Professor's Dream:
a symposium of principal monuments of
ancient and modern times, drawn to the same
scale', c. 1848*

This is a light, preparatory pencil sketch
for the large coloured drawing that
Cockerell exhibited to great acclaim at
the Royal Academy of Arts, London, in
1848. Professor of Architecture at the
Royal Academy, Cockerell was also greatly
respected as a Classical archaeologist, thus
the preponderance of ancient temples in
the drawing. The composition is balanced
by a triangle of three large domes:
Florence Cathedral (right), St Peter's,
Rome (centre) and St Paul's, London
(left), of which Cockerell was Surveyor.

97.
Andrea Palladio (1508–80)
*Idealised reconstruction of the forum and
sanctuary of Fortuna Primigenia, Palestrina
(ancient Praeneste), Italy, c. 1560*

The ruins of Praeneste, the ancient Roman
temple complex 35 miles east of Rome,
provided Italian Renaissance architects
with a rich source of inspiration and an
outstanding model for their own work.
Andrea Palladio, perhaps the most
influential figure in the history of
architecture, studied and measured the
remains of the hillside site and made
drawings in a faithful attempt to
reconstruct its lost glory. He then created
a series of architectural fantasies,
of which this is the most famous,
exaggerating and enhancing the columned
terraces and piazzas leading to the great
circular temple at its summit. The scholar
Douglas Lewis views this drawing as a
'hallucinatory elaboration', Palladio's
'megalomaniacal *tour de force*'.

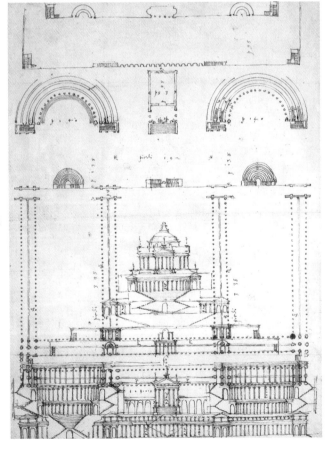

41.
Raymond Erith (1904–73) and
Quinlan Terry (b. 1937)
Drawing by Quinlan Terry
House of Worship, Tehran, 1972–77

This temple for worshippers of the
Baha'i faith practising in Tehran was
commissioned in the early 1970s. It was
the last collaboration between Raymond
Erith and Quinlan Terry as Erith died
halfway through the project. The whole
scheme was drawn up and had started on
site, when the Iranian revolution brought
work to a stop. The design of the temple is
based on the numbers nine and nineteen,
mystical to the Baha'is, and combines forms
taken from early Florentine Renaissance
churches fused with elements of Islamic
detailing.

1.
Robert Adam (1728–92)
*A landscape fantasy showing castles and
domed city, c. 1777–87*

Robert Adam was the most fashionable
British architect of the late eighteenth
century, specialising in country and town
houses with highly ornamented interiors.
During the last decades of his life, even
with a busy office to run, Adam found time
to produce a series of picturesque
landscape fantasies for his own pleasure.
The castles hint at the Scottish fortresses
he knew from his youth; the domed
buildings dipping down to the mountain
river are like the lost Roman cities Adam
had studied in Italy and Dalmatia in the
1750s, gaining the specialised knowledge
required to become a successful architect.

91.
Takehiko Nagakura (b. 1962)
The Unbuilt Monuments
Monument to the Third International
(Vladimir Tatlin, 1919), 1999 (still)

Shortly after the Russian Revolution,
the Soviet artist and founder of the
Constructivist movement, Vladimir Tatlin,
proposed a monument to commemorate
the Third International (the international
Communist organisation founded by Lenin
in 1919 and dissolved in 1943). Although
the tower was never built, Tatlin's dream was
to violently insert it into the Classical centre
of St Petersburg. *Tatlin's Tower*, as it is often
referred to, is widely known by architects
and historians, but only through its
designer's mysterious description, his
abstract drawings and a sculptural model.
After conducting research into the
availability of structural materials and
technologies in the early 1900s, Nagakura's
production team added construction details
to the original design to derive a convincing
appearance. Synthetic computer images of
the tower are then superimposed with live
footage of contemporary St Petersburg.

90.
Takehiko Nagakura (b. 1962)
The Unbuilt Monuments
The Danteum (Guiseppe Terragni/Pietro
Lingeri, 1938), 1998 (still)

Like the digital reconstruction of *Tatlin's,*
Tower shown above, this still is taken from a
series of short films in which the architect
and teacher Takahiko Nagakura uses
historical designs and computer generated
imagery to recreate seminal unrealised
Modernist projects. Designed for
Mussolini to be located on a site close to
the Roman Colosseum, *The Danteum* was
conceived as a monument to the poet
Alighieri Dante (1265–1321). The plan
was abandoned following Mussolini's
defeat in the Second World War, though
detailed plans and drawings survived.
The building's allegorical organisation
of space is modelled after Dante's spatial
description in his *Divine Comedy*. Here,
Nagakura uses a computer graphic
simulation of one long uninterrupted
camera movement, set at eye level, to imply
the experience of walking through *The*
Danteum from the entrance through the
chambers of Hell, Purgatory and Paradise,
shown here.

2.
The Adventure Company/Wanadoo
(est. 1996)
The Mystery of the Mummy, 2003

Inspired by Sir Arthur Conan Doyle's
Adventures of Sherlock Holmes, this computer
game transposes the player to turn-of-the-
century England where he or she is cast as
the famous detective investigating the
disappearance of Lord Montcalfe – an
archaeologist specialising in ancient
Egyptology – and an Egyptian Mummy. In
order to solve the mystery, the player must
navigate through the four levels of
Montcalfe's labyrinthine mansion – which
also serves as a private museum. The
design of the graphics for *The Mystery of the
Mummy* reconfigures convincing period
detail, inspired by Victorian photographs,
and architectural and interior design
schemes into a claustrophobic virtual maze
of hidden chambers, alcoves, niches,
compartments and conundrums. The 360
degree interface allows for panoramic and
floor to ceiling sweeps which divulge the
spatial and atmospheric qualities of the
environment to full advantage.

100.
Giovanni Pastrone (1883–1959)
Cabiria, 1914 (still)

Among the most ambitious and influential
of silent films *Cabiria* tells the epic story of
its eponymous heroine, a Roman slave girl
kidnapped as a child and sold into slavery
in Carthage at the beginning of the Second
Punic War (218–201 BC). The director,
Giovanni Pastrone, obsessed over historical
detail and spent months researching
period clothing, buildings and décor
before production began.

20.
Alexander Carse (*fl.* 1790–1838)
View of the Willow Cathedral, 1792

'Old Carse', as Alexander Carse was known, was a watercolour artist of everyday scenes. Here he records a craftsman constructing a 'cathedral' made of ash posts and willow rods, an experiment by the Scottish scientist Sir James Hall as evidence to his theory that Gothic architecture evolved from simple wattle buildings that came to be reproduced in stone. Hall published the results of his investigations in *Origin, Principles, and History of Gothic Architecture* in 1813.

130.
William Walcot (1874–1943)
Reconstruction of the Temple of Diana, Ephesus, Turkey, 1923

Trained as an architect, Walcot is best known as a perspectivist and for creating conjectural reconstructions such as this of antique buildings. Walcot's vision of the *Temple of Diana at Ephesus*, one of the seven wonders of the ancient world, is colourful and artistic, an atmospheric interpretation of the painter's formidable scholarly knowledge.

104.
Arthur Beresford Pite (1861–1934)
Competition design for a 'West-End Club House', for the Soane Medallion Prize, 1882

Working in a style reminiscent of the Renaissance artist Albrecht Dürer, the 21-year-old Beresford Pite drew this extraordinarily atmospheric and virtuosic perspective for a student competition. It was a rebellious drawing; London West End clubs have always been dignified Classical buildings, not forbidding Medieval fortresses. The judges, obviously impressed, awarded Pite the prize. Pite's later works were never so fantastic, although much admired, as with his Christ Church, Brixton Road, London.

In Memoriam

108.
John Pollard Seddon (1827–1906) and
Edward Beckitt Lamb (1857–1934)
*Design for the Imperial Monumental Halls and
Tower, Westminster, London,* 1904 (detail)

As the dead heroes of the Victorian
period began to pile up, space ran out
in Westminster Abbey for their memorials.
As a solution, the architects Seddon and
Lamb proposed this addition: an
enormous Hall of Valhalla with a Gothic
tower to out-soar even the famous Clock
Tower on Barry's Houses of Parliament.
This is one of four large bird's-eye views
of the scheme.

23.
William Chambers (1723–96)
Design for a mausoleum in ruins, c. 1751

For whom this tomb was intended is not
known; but in 1751, Chambers designed
a mausoleum to the memory of Frederick,
Prince of Wales. Chambers often favoured
this method of presenting buildings in
semi-ruin. At the time he made this
drawing, he was living in Rome and
studying Classical antiquities.

42.
FAT (Fashion, Architecture, Taste)
(est. 1995)
Princess Diana Memorial Bridge, 1998

This proposal for a pedestrian bridge over
the river Thames links London's St Paul's
Cathedral to Tate Modern, the site of
Foster and Partners' now infamous 'wobbly'
Millenium Bridge. The bridge incorporates
a slice of Northamptonshire countryside,
taken from Althorp Park, the seat of
Princess Diana's family, the Spencers. The
strip of picturesque parkland contrasts with
the financial and cultural centre of
London. It provides an opportunity for
contemplation in a rural setting and also
a place for laying floral tributes to the late
Princess. The lyrics to Elton John's tribute
song, 'Candle in the Wind', are carved into
the stone structure of the bridge. FAT's
scheme considers the bridge as an
opportunity for an experience rather
than a display of technical ingenuity,
a destination as much as a journey.

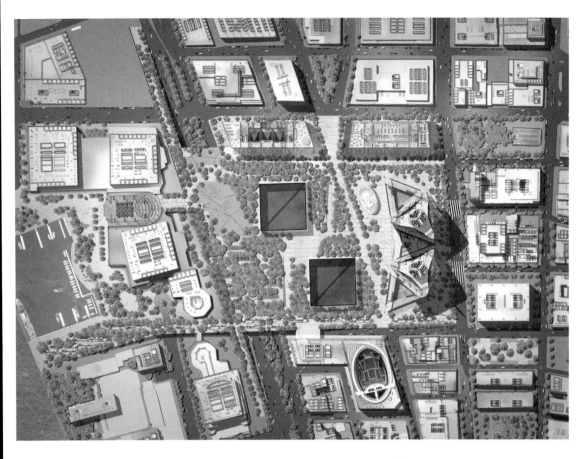

47.
Foster and Partners (est. 1967)
Rebuilding of the World Trade Center Site, 2002

This was one of nine proposals from seven
teams of international architects in the
competition to replace the World Trade
Center destroyed in the terrorist attacks
of September 11, 2001. With the need to
respect the history of the site, Foster's
proposal retained the areas of the two
original towers' footprints as memorial
parks for private remembrance and
reflection. The design of the towers
themselves is based on triangular
geometries described by the architects
as 'cross-cultural symbols of harmony,
wisdom, purity, unity and strength'.
Constructed to 'kiss at three points', thus
maximising escape routes in the event of
an emergency, the interiors of these
'twinned towers' are also broken down
into village-like clusters, each with its own
tree-filled atrium. The building's raking
corners offer the opportunity for
funiculars to transport the public vertically
up the building.

In Memoriam

71.
Hector Horeau (1801–72)
*Design, unexecuted, for a monument to
Sir Robert Peel*, 1850

The eccentric French architect Hector
Horeau designed this monument to Sir
Robert Peel, the Prime Minister who had
recently died from falling from his horse.
Horeau was an avid Anglophile and this
was his homage to an Englishman greatly
mourned. The statue of Peel is raised
over the water, like an ancient Colossus
of Rhodes, a protector of those who pass
beneath. Set on a decorated cast-iron
structure (reminiscent of the yet-to-be-
designed Eiffel Tower) the memorial
spanned, but was not attached to, the bridge.

59.
Thomas Affleck Greeves (1917–97)
Capriccio entitled 'Design for a monument to commemorate the passing of the good old days of architecture', 1951

Thomas Greeves caught the light-heartedness of the 1951 Festival of Britain in his humorous design for a building with Dutch gables in the Queen Anne style of the 1870s. This was a winning entry in a competition organised by the Architects Benevolent Society. Sir Osbert Lancaster, a cartoonist and writer, was one of the assessors.

43.
John Flaxman (1755–1826)
Design for 'A Mausoleum for Ching Chong Chow, Emperor of China', 1777

In jest, the young sculptor John Flaxman has pencilled onto this drawing that it is a 'mausoleum adorned with colossal sculpture being an attempt at something in a New style', intended for the exhibition at the Royal Academy in 1777. This was the year in which the architect John Soane had shown his design for a mausoleum to the memory of James King, a friend who had recently drowned. It has been therefore suggested that Flaxman is mocking Soane's gesture as maudlin and the style as pretentious. At this time, Flaxman was designing for the potter Josiah Wedgwood, so China may well have been on his mind.

In Memoriam

64.
Louis Hellman (b. 1936)
Thatcher Monument, 1998

At first glance a striking Expressionist
monument to the end of an era, this
design reveals an even spikier character
when looked at sideways: the profile of the
'Iron Lady' herself. This design is a wry
comment on Lady Thatcher's often-quoted
barnstorming conference speech when she
adamantly stated that in policy terms 'the
Lady's not for turning'. At the same time
the monument lampoons Thatcher for the
architectural legacy of her premiership
which, as Hellman points out, lay in
'suburban supermarkets pretending to be
rural barns, "yuppie" housing in converted
sold-off council houses and Canary Wharf,
a monument to ruthless *laissez-faire*
gigantism (through a three billion pound
public subsidy "incentive").'

61.
Thomas Harrison (1744–1829)
Design for a military and naval monument,
1814

In response to the Napoleonic Wars,
Harrison produced this cool and austere
drawing for a riverside mausoleum for the
British conquerors. Dead heroes, it
appears, prefer an ancient Greco-Roman
heaven, a result of Harrison's architectural
studies in Rome during the 1770s, where
his talent had come to the attention of the
Pope. Although the monument was not
built, Harrison, a Chester-based architect,
added greatly to the growing metropolitan
magnificence of Manchester and Liverpool
with many churches, theatres and libraries.
He also specialised in bridges, which
explains the view of the building seen
below a bridge arch.

56.
Ernö Goldfinger (1902–87)
*Competition design for a memorial chapel for
a cardinal, for Prix de la Fondation Rougevin,
1926*

A heavenly finger of light illuminates
the kneeling figure of a cardinal in
Goldfinger's Ecole des Beaux Arts student
drawing. Large and impressive, student
work at the Ecole in the 1920s still followed
in the nineteenth-century tradition of
formal Classicism. Goldfinger would soon
make the leap into the new modern style
with one of his first commissions, a shop
in London's Mayfair for the queen of
cosmetics, Helena Rubenstein. Later in
his career, having moved permanently
to Britain from his native Hungary, he
became respected by some, reviled by
others, for designing powerful concrete
structures such as Trellick Tower (1967)
in North Kensington, London.

113.
John Soane (1753–1837)
Copy by Charles James Richardson
(1806–1871)
*'Architectural visions of early fancy in the gay
morning of youth and dreams in the evening
of life', c. 1825*

As Sir John Soane, architect of the Bank
of England, grew older, he became
nostalgic and melancholic about the
unbuilt designs of his youth. So he
commissioned his favoured perspective
artist, J.M. Gandy, to create a large
watercolour showing a collage of his early
work, to which he added a wistful title,
inscribed on a flat boulder on the lower
right of the drawing. This is a small copy,
made by one of Soane's pupils; the original
hangs in Sir John Soane's Museum,
Lincoln's Inn Fields, London (fig.6).

85.
Tom Mellor (1914–94)
*Capriccio of Notre-Dame du Haut, Ronchamp,
France in ruins*, 1981

The French architect, Le Corbusier,
was a giant of twentieth-century modern
architecture. His pilgrimage church
at Ronchamp, completed in 1955, is
considered one of his finest buildings.
The architect-artist Tom Mellor, with great
admiration, has nevertheless turned it into
a ruin, in the style of such eighteenth-
century masters as William Chambers.
It is Mellor's *memento mori* for architecture,
a sobering reminder that not only has the
Modernism of Le Corbusier passed away,
but that nothing, no matter how beautiful
and substantial, lasts forever.

58.
Francis Goodwin (1784–1835)
Perspective by Thomas Allom
Design for 'National Cemetery', Primrose Hill, London, c. 1830

This miniature drawing by the architect and watercolourist Thomas Allom, was an unsolicited proposal by Francis Goodwin for creating a great cemetery overlooking London. It was a piece of speculation done in the hope that the recently formed General Cemetery Company would take it up. They didn't. Goodwin's model was Père-Lachaise cemetery in Paris, with its avenues and grand monuments.

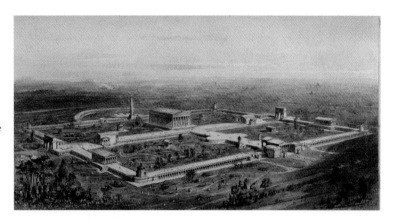

95.
Claes Oldenburg (b. 1929)
London Knees (Edition of 120, signed and numbered), 1966–68

This monument to the mini-skirt was designed by the Swedish-born sculptor, Claes Oldenburg, while visiting London in 1966. Reflecting on the work some thirty years after its conception Oldenburg said, 'London Knees [...] was a very contemporary phenomenon due to the recent invention of the mini-skirt. It is difficult now to imagine how revolutionary this paradoxical combination of a masculine voyeurism and feminine liberation seemed at the time. The architectural and fetishistic functions of knees were accentuated by the fashion of wearing boots with the mini which created a sharply demarcated area of the body suitable for objectification.'

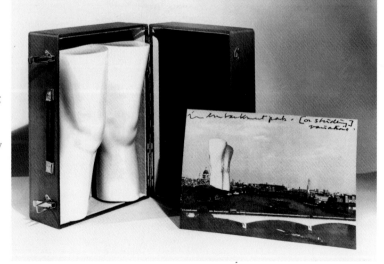

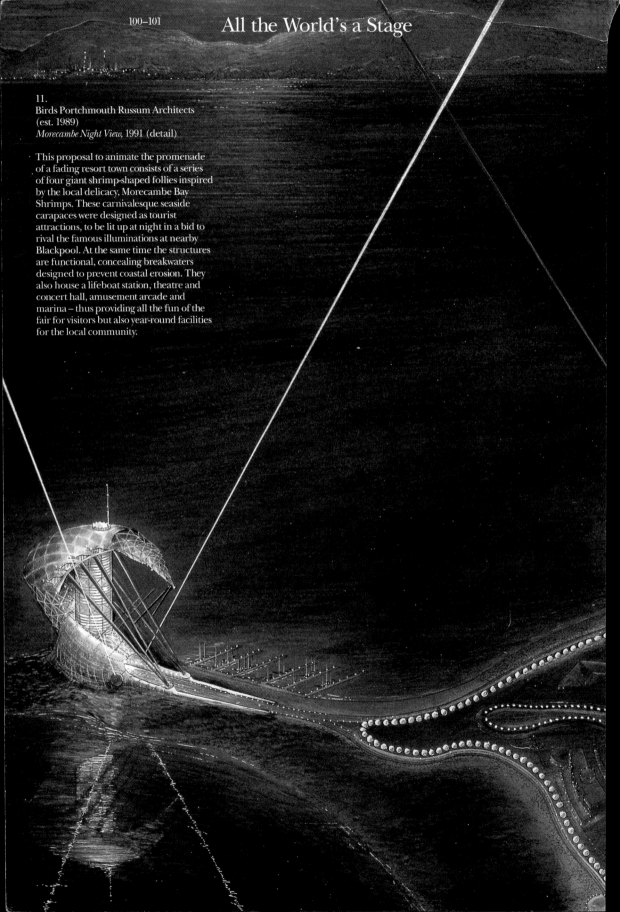

11.
Birds Portchmouth Russum Architects
(est. 1989)
Morecambe Night View, 1991 (detail)

This proposal to animate the promenade
of a fading resort town consists of a series
of four giant shrimp-shaped follies inspired
by the local delicacy, Morecambe Bay
Shrimps. These carnivalesque seaside
carapaces were designed as tourist
attractions, to be lit up at night in a bid to
rival the famous illuminations at nearby
Blackpool. At the same time the structures
are functional, concealing breakwaters
designed to prevent coastal erosion. They
also house a lifeboat station, theatre and
concert hall, amusement arcade and
marina – thus providing all the fun of the
fair for visitors but also year-round facilities
for the local community.

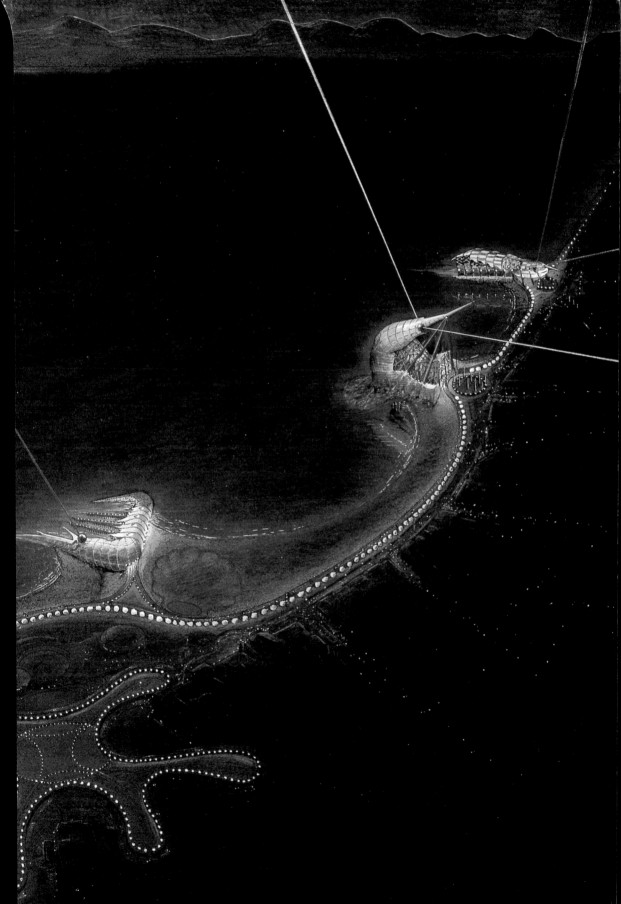

3.
John Alexander (1888–1974)
Design for an unidentified cinema in northeast England, c. 1935

During the 1930s, the ultimate escape from workaday life was a night at the picture-show. Designers, such as John Alexander of Newcastle-upon-Tyne, heightened the theatrical experience by creating cinema interiors decorated in fantasy themes, usually incorporating exotic locations or historical subjects. Appropriate for a chilly northern English town, this design is of a hot Spanish setting.

105.
Cedric Price (1934–2003)
Interior View for the Fun Palace, 1961–65

This huge, steel-framed structure was designed to provide a completely flexible envelope to contain a programme of music, theatre and dance. The client was the visionary director Joan Littlewood, a passionate believer in community and political theatre, and it was intended, in her words, to be a 'laboratory of fun'. Its moveable stages, walls and walkways, roofs and screens were designed to be serviced by cranes and helicopters. Price believed that alongside the three dimensions of space, time is the fourth dimension of design and through projects such as this explored architecture's ability to nurture new ideas and social change. Littlewood's *Fun Palace* was never built due to lack of funding and for most of its life her company was based at the Theatre Royal in Stratford, a dilapidated palace of varieties in East London. Nevertheless, the *Fun Palace* project proved highly influential on the work of later architects, most notably on Richard Rogers and Renzo Piano's winning scheme for the Centre Pompidou in Paris (1971–77).

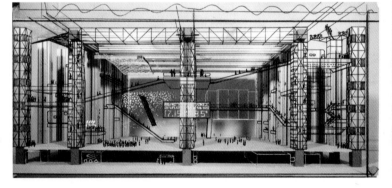

31.
Corbett, Harrison & MacMurray, Hood &
Fouilhoux and C. Howard Crane
Exterior perspective attributed to John
Wenrich
*Design for International Music Hall and Opera
House, Hyde Park Corner, London, c. 1935*

This virtuosic pencil drawing comes from
a series of designs for a proposed music
centre of which little else is known. The
architects were the same group that had
created Radio City Music Hall in New
York in 1932. The site at Hyde Park
Corner is where the Lanesborough Hotel
now stands and which, at the time of the
project, was St George's Hospital. The
building would have been London's
most extravagant Art Deco creation.

VIEW FROM WELLINGTON ARCH
DESIGN A

32.
Corbett, Harrison & MacMurray, Hood &
Fouilhoux and C. Howard Crane
Interior perspective of Grand Foyer
attributed to John Wenrich
*Design for International Music Hall and Opera
House, Hyde Park Corner, London, c. 1935*

The American-designed interiors of this
monumental entertainment centre were
near-identical copies of Radio City Music
Hall in New York, and are therefore
probably also by its interior decorator
Donald Deskey. The Grand Foyer was
to be hung with 29-foot long chandeliers.

GRAND FOYER

All the World's a Stage

50.
Antonio Galli Bibiena (1700–74)
Stage set design for royal apartments, c. 1728

Antonio was a member of the famous Galli
Bibiena family, which dominated stage
design across Europe in the eighteenth-
century and specialised in creating sets
of exuberant architectural fantasy. Such
inventions usually were created for wealthy
royal courts, as an exaggeration of the
pomp, ostentation and display of the
audience itself.

52.
Guiseppe Galli Bibiena (1695–1757)
Stage set design for a domed palace, c. 1723

This set design shows fantasy at its most
Baroque, as a confection to overwhelm
theatre audiences and as an appropriate
backdrop for the highly exaggerated
movements and dialogues of the actors.
The stage illusion would be created by a
combination of painted canvas backcloths
and wooden scenery, layered to increase
the effect of the perspective and often
made moveable by mechanised wing
changes. Guiseppe travelled throughout
Austria and Germany creating opera sets,
firework displays and wedding decorations,
working closely with his father, Fernando.

51.
Giovanni Carlo Galli Bibiena (1713–60)
*Stage set design for 'La Clemenza di Tito',
Act I, scene 2, c. 1755*

This set was for an opera staged in
Lisbon for the birthday of Joseph I,
King of Portugal, in 1755. The music
was by Antonio Mazzoni. The setting is
Michelangelo's Rome reinterpreted
with startling swagger. All the formal lines
of Michelangelo's Capitoline Palaces and
the great external stairs have been altered
exuberantly in a high Baroque manner,
curving and bowing.

73.
Inigo Jones (1573–1652)
*Design for a temporary ceremonial structure for
a queen, c. 1619*

This freehand drawing by Inigo Jones,
the leading architect of the early English
Renaissance, may be his design for Queen
Anne of Denmark's catafalque, the
processional float carried through the
streets at her funeral. The consort of James I
died in 1619 and there is a record of Jones
having been commissioned for such a
structure, a combination of the architect's
talents for architectural design and stage
sets. Only a few years earlier, in 1616, Jones
had begun to build the Queen's House in
Greenwich for Anne – although she died
before it was completed.

List of Works

All measurements are in cm and are height x width x depth. Page references are to illustrations in this book.

All works are courtesy RIBA Library Drawings Collection, unless otherwise stated.

1 (p.85)
Robert Adam
A landscape fantasy showing castles and domed city, c. 1777–87
brown pen and coloured washes on paper; 35 x 47

2 (p.87)
The Adventure Company/Wanadoo
The Mystery of the Mummy, 2003
computer game; dimensions variable
Software © 2003 Wanadoo Edition/ DreamCatcherInteractive Inc.
Developed by Frogwares © Frogwares 2004

3 (p.102)
John Alexander
Design for an unidentified cinema in northeast England, c. 1935
pencil, gouache, silver and gold paint and coloured washes on paper; 53 x 65

4 (p.42)
Alsop Architects
The Fourth Grace, 2002
polystyrene and plastic detailed model in three parts; 66 x 90 x 80
Courtesy Alsop Architects
© Alsop Architects Ltd. 2004. Image by Virtual Artworks

5 (p.30)
Anchor Blocks; F.A.D. Richter & Co. (Rudolstadte, Thuringia, Germany)
Anchor Blocks, c. 1920s
Book of designs for Anchor Blocks No. 206: *Bungalow Box, c. 1920s*
Book of designs for Anchor Blocks No. 208: *Suburban Box, c. 1920s*
Anchor Blocks: compositional stone (sand, chalk and linseed oil, natural colouring); box size 5 x 23 x 32.5

6 (p.70)
Michael Anderson, director
1984, 1956
film still; dimensions variable
Produced by N. Peter Rathvon
Screenplay by William P. Templeton and Ralph Bettinson (based on the novel *1984* by George Orwell)
Photo: courtesy British Film Institute

7 (p.43)
Ove Nyquist Arup
Sketch designs for Opera House, Sydney, Australia, 1961
pencil on paper; 26 x 153

8 (p.58)
Asymptote: Hani Rashid and Lisa Anne Couture
New York Virtual Stock Exchange, 1997–2000
computer-generated animation on DVD; running time: 3 minutes, 48 seconds
Courtesy Hani Rashid, Asymptote
© NYSE/SIAC/ASYMPTOTE 2004

9 (p.54)
Charles Barry
Design for a Palace of Government Offices, Whitehall, London, 1858
pen and coloured washes on paper; 78 x 144.5

10 (p.53)
John Belcher
Perspective by William Bingham McGuiness
Competition design, unexecuted, for the South Kensington Museum, now the Victoria and Albert Museum, London, 1891
pen, gouache and wash on paper; 101 x 64.5

11 (pp.100–101)
Birds Portchmouth Russum Architects
Morecambe Night View, 1991
crayon ink on film; 86 x 62.5
Courtesy Birds Portchmouth Russum Architects
© Birds Portchmouth Russum Architects 2004

12
Birds Portchmouth Russum Architects
Morecambe Seafront-Construction View, 1991
ink drawing of construction; 133 x 62.5
Courtesy Birds Portchmouth Russum Architects
© Birds Portchmouth Russum Architects 2004

13 (p.78)
Birds Portchmouth Russum Architects
Croydon, The Future, 1993
hand-coloured ink on film with photomontage; 175 x 140 x 10
Courtesy Birds Portchmouth Russum Architects
© Birds Portchmouth Russum Architects 2004

14 (p.54)
Etienne-Louis Boullée
Design for a Metropolitan Cathedral, 1782
pen and wash on paper; 33 x 63

15 (pp.82–83)
Henry Carlton Bradshaw
'The Temple of Fortune and its surroundings restored', Palestrina (ancient Praeneste), Italy, 1919
pencil, pen, gouache and coloured washes on paper; 57 x 142.5

16 (pp.82–83)
Henry William Brewer
Panorama of *'London in the time of Henry VIII'*, 1887
pen on paper; 42 x 151

17 (p.59)
W. Bridges
'A plan and elevation for a bridge over the River Avon at the Rocks of St Vincent from Sion Row, Clifton to Leigh Down near Bristol Hot Well', 1793
pen, pencil and coloured washes on paper; 27 x 37

18 (pp.68–69)
David Butler, director
Just Imagine, 1930
film still; dimensions variable
Produced by Twentieth Century Fox
'JUST IMAGINE' © 1930 Twentieth Century Fox. All rights reserved.
Photo: courtesy British Film Institute

19 (p.62)
Stefan Buzas
Competition design, unexecuted, for the 'Vertical Feature', 1951 Festival of Britain, South Bank, London, c. 1950
coloured pastel on paper; 67 x 34

20 (p.88)
Alexander Carse
View of the Willow Cathedral, 1792
watercolour on paper; 20.5 x 25.5

21 (p.43)
Eduardo Fernando Catalano
Drawings to illustrate the structures of warped surfaces and columns, 1952–57
pen and pencil with crayon added on paper; 33 x 45.5

22
Eduardo Fernando Catalano
Drawings to illustrate the structures of warped surfaces and columns, 1952–57
pen and pencil with crayon added on paper; 33 x 45.5

23 (p.92)
William Chambers
Design for a mausoleum in ruins, c. 1751
pen and brown, grey and pink washes on paper; 43.5 x 33.5

24 (p.30)
Max Clenndining
Perspective by Ralph Adron
Design for an interior, made for The Daily Telegraph *newspaper*, 1968
acrylic paint under plastic film; 33 x 43
Courtesy V&A Images/V&A Museum

25 (p.44)
James Clephan
*Design, unexecuted, for an elevated railway,
London, c.* 1845
print; 33.5 x 24

26 (p.84)
Charles Robert Cockerell
*Preliminary design for 'The Professor's Dream:
a symposium of principal monuments of ancient
and modern times, drawn to the same scale',
c.* 1848
pencil on paper; 57 x 87.5

27 (p.56)
Constant (Constant A. Nieuwenhuys)
View of New Babylonian sectors, 1971
inkjet print from original; 50 x 56
Courtesy Municipal Museum, The Hague

28 (p.52)
Peter Cook; Archigram
Plug-In City; Max. pressure area, 1964
black-and-white photographic print (from
original line drawing on tracing paper)
with applied colour film
Courtesy Archigram Archive
Peter Cook; Archigram © 1964

29 (p.45)
Peter Cook
Design for Solar City, 1980
print, coloured; 60.5 x 60.5

30 (p.62)
Peter Cook
*Design for Sleektower and Verandah Tower,
Brisbane, Queensland, Australia,* 1984
print, coloured; 101 x 73.5

31 (p.103)
Corbett, Harrison & MacMurray, Hood
& Fouilhoux and C. Howard Crane
Exterior perspective attributed to John
Wenrich
*Design for International Music Hall and Opera
House, Hyde Park Corner, London, c.* 1935
pencil, crayon and gouache on paper;
55 x 72.5

32 (p.103)
Corbett, Harrison & MacMurray, Hood &
Fouilhoux and C. Howard Crane
Interior perspective of Grand Foyer
attributed to John Wenrich
*Design for International Music Hall and Opera
House, Hyde Park Corner, London, c.* 1935.
gouache and gold paint on paper; 55 x 72.5

33 (p.74)
George Dance junior
'View of London, with the Improvements', 1802
print; 58 x 86

34 (p.73)
Balkrishna V. Doshi
*'Concept' design for Vidhyadhar Nagar, Jaipur,
Rajasthan, India,* 1980
silkscreen print; 70.5 x 55

35
Balkrishna V. Doshi
*'Vignette' design for Vidhyadhar Nagar, Jaipur,
Rajasthan, India,* 1980
silkscreen print; 70.5 x 55

36 (p.44)
Ronald Aver Duncan
Design for the 'House of the Future', Ideal
Home *exhibition, Olympia, Hammersmith
and Fulham, London,* 1928
pen and wash on paper; 35.5 x 28

37 (p.72)
EA Games
SimCity™ originally designed by Will
Wright at Maxis, 1989
SimCity™ *4,* 2003
computer game; dimensions variable
SimCity™ image used with permission of
Electronic Arts Inc. © 1997–2004 Electronic
Arts Inc. All Rights Reserved. *SimCity*™ is a
trademark of Electronic Arts Inc. in the US
and/or other countries

38 (p.67)
Elgo Plastics Inc., Chicago, Illinois, USA
American Skyline, first manufactured 1956
plastic; box size 33 x 45.5 x 5

39 (p.71)
Maurice Elvey, director
High Treason, 1928
film extract transferred to DVD; running
time: 1 minute
Produced by Gaumont
Screenplay by L'Estrange Fawcett based
on a play by Noel Pemberton-Billing
Image supplied courtesy of Carlton
International Media Limited
Photo: courtesy British Film Institute

40 (p.63)
English (late fifteenth or early sixteenth-
century master)
Design for a tower with turrets, c. 1490–1510
pen with coloured washes on vellum;
49 x 19.5

41 (p.85)
Raymond Erith and Quinlan Terry
Drawing by Quinlan Terry
House of Worship, Tehran, 1972–77
pencil on paper; 105 x 157
Courtesy Lord Alistair McAlpine of
West Green
Photo: courtesy David Grandorge

42 (p.92)
FAT (Fashion, Architecture, Taste)
Princess Diana Memorial Bridge, 1998
computer-generated image shown
as digital print; dimensions variable
Courtesy FAT
© FAT 1997. Image by Will Lee

43 (p.95)
John Flaxman
*Design for 'A Mausoleum for Ching Chong
Chow, Emperor of China',* 1777
pencil on paper; 19.5 x 25.5
Courtesy V&A Images/V&A Museum

44 (p.31)
Foreign Office Architects
Virtual House, 1997
computer-generated image shown
as digital print; dimensions variable
Courtesy Foreign Office Architects; Farshid
Moussavi and Alejandro Zaera-Polo with
Monica Company, Kenichi Matsuzawa,
Jordi Mansilla, Manuel Monterde,
Manuel Perez
© Foreign Office Architects 1997

45 (p.59)
Foreign Office Architects
The Bundle Tower, 2001–02
computer-generated image shown
as digital print; dimensions variable
Courtesy Foreign Office Architects; Farshid
Moussavi and Alejandro Zaera-Polo with
Daniel Lopez-Perez, Erhard An-He
Kinzelbach, Edouard Cabay,
Chu Ka Wing Kelvin
© Foreign Office Architects 2001

46 (p.63)
Foster and Partners
M Tower, Tokyo, 1993
perspex, plastic, wood; 90 x 43.5 x 146.5
Courtesy Foster and Partners
© Foster and Partners 2004

47 (p.93)
Foster and Partners
Rebuilding of the World Trade Center Site, 2002
perspex, plastic, wood; 120 x 40 x 40
diameter base
Courtesy Foster and Partners
© Foster and Partners 2004

48 (pp.50–51)
Freedom Ship International Inc
Freedom Ship, 2002
computer-generated image shown
as digital print; dimensions variable
Courtesy Freedom Ship International Inc.
Chief Design Architect, Kevin Schopfer,
Originator, Norman E. Nixon

List of Works

49 (p.45)
Richard Buckminster Fuller
Sketch for a geodesic dome, inscribed 'To Tom/ with affectionate regard/Bucky Fuller Jan 29 1972', 1972
pen with black and red marker on brown envelope; 30.5 x 24

50 (p.104)
Antonio Galli Bibiena
Stage set design for royal apartments,
c. 1728
pen and wash on paper; 38 x 42.5

51 (p.105)
Giovanni Carlo Galli Bibiena
Stage set design for 'La Clemenza di Tito', Act I, scene 2, c. 1755
pen and grey and brown washes on paper;
20 x 26

52 (p.104)
Guiseppe Galli Bibiena
Stage set design for a domed palace, c. 1723
pen and grey and brown washes on paper;
33.5 x 48.5

53 (p.46)
Stephen Geary
Design for Cosmos Institute, Leicester Square, London, c. 1830
print with coloured washes added on paper;
20 x 25.5

54
Stephen Geary
Design for Cosmos Institute, Leicester Square, London, c. 1830
print with coloured washes added on paper;
20 x 25.5

55 (p.31)
German (maker unknown, probably made in Munich)
'Moderne Baukunst', c. 1830s–40s
wood, with applied printed surface, hand-coloured; box size 4 x 20.5 x 16

56 (p.97)
Ernö Goldfinger
Competition design for a memorial chapel for a cardinal, for Prix de la Fondation Rougevin, 1926
pencil, pen, wash, gouache and gold paint on paper; 99 x 53

57 (p.32)
Ernö Goldfinger
Drawing showing a typical modern type of urban flat, 1942
print with coloured washes added on paper;
33 x 49

58 (p.99)
Francis Goodwin
Perspective by Thomas Allom
Design for 'National Cemetery', Primrose Hill, London, c. 1830
pen, gouache and watercolour on paper;
11 x 21

59 (p.95)
Thomas Affleck Greeves
Capriccio entitled 'Design for a monument to commemorate the passing of the good old days of architecture', 1951
pen, pencil and coloured washes on paper;
53 x 38

60 (p.76)
Zaha Hadid
The Peak Club, Hong Kong, 1982–83
gouache on paper; 120.5 x 151.5
Design Team: Zaha Hadid with M. Wolfson, J. Dunn, M. van der Waals, N. Ayoubi
Presentation: M. Wolfson, A. Standing, N. Lee, M. Galway
Structural Engineers: Ove Arup & Partners with David Thomlinson

61 (p.96)
Thomas Harrison
Design for a military and naval monument, 1814
pen and wash on paper; 27.4 x 63.5

62 (p.46)
Joseph Hartland
'Plan for removing houses. As adopted in the United States by Letter Patent', 1833
pen and coloured washes on paper; 44 x 33

63 (p.70)
Hayes Davidson
Fast Forward, 2001
computer-enhanced film on DVD; running time: 5 minutes, 31 seconds
Courtesy Hayes Davidson
© Hayes Davidson 2001

64 (p.96)
Louis Hellman
Thatcher Monument, 1998
ink, pencil and watercolour on paper;
30 x 19.5
Courtesy Louis Hellman

65
Louis Hellman
A Mansion for a Monarch, 2003
ink and film on tracing paper; 21.5 x 23.5
Courtesy Louis Hellman

66
Louis Hellman
A Pad for a Prince, 2003
ink and film on tracing paper; 21.5 x 23.5
Courtesy Louis Hellman

67 (p.32)
Louis Hellman
A Palace for a Premier, 2003
ink and film on tracing paper; 21.5 x 23.5
Courtesy Louis Hellman

68
Louis Hellman
A Residence for a President, 2003
ink and film on tracing paper; 21.5 x 23.5
Courtesy Louis Hellman

69 (p.42)
Ron Herron; Archigram
W.C. 'Moving', 1964
ink sketch on paper, 215 x 125
Courtesy Simon Herron

70 (p.57)
Charles Holden
Perspective by A. Bryett
Design, known as 'Spiral Scheme II', partially executed, for the University of London, Bloomsbury, London, 1933
pen, pencil and gouache and coloured washes on paper; 47 x 100

71 (p.94)
Hector Horeau
Design, unexecuted, for a monument to Sir Robert Peel, 1850
pen on paper; 37 x 15.5

72 (p.74)
Helmut Jacoby
Town Park, Water Carpet and Cone Area, 1976
pencil on paper; 86.5 x 38
Courtesy Professor Derek Walker, Chief Architect and Planner, Milton Keynes
Design: Derek Walker, Andrew Mahaddie, Anthony NG. Rendering Helmut Jacoby
© Derek Walker 2004
Photo: John Donat

73 (p.105)
Inigo Jones
Design for a temporary ceremonial structure for a queen, c. 1619
pen on paper; 30 x 18

74 (p.39)
James Kennedy-Hawkes
'Sketch design for holiday cottage on the East Coast', 1941
pencil and colour washes on squared paper;
21 x 29.5

75 (p.47)
William Low
Design for 'Channel Tunnel Railway', 1868
print with coloured washes added on paper;
27.5 x 75.5

76 (p.35)
Berthold Lubetkin
Peter Yates, draughtsman
Alternative designs, unexecuted, for prefabricated house fronts, for the 100 House Scheme, Thornhill Gill Housing, Peterlee, County Durham, c. 1949
various media including pencil, pen, gouache, watercolour and some collage on paper; 12 sheets, 28 x 25 each

77 (p.34)
Edwin Lutyens
'Castle-in-the-air' sketchbook, showing an imaginary palace entitled 'Port Fleuviale de Circonstance', c. 1895–96
pencil and colour washes on paper; 13 x 18.5, sheet size; p. 2 of 28 pp canvas bound sketchbook

78 (p.35)
Edwin Lutyens
Design for house, Gravesend, Kent for Captain E.W.S. Day, 1919
pen, pencil and coloured crayon on paper; 14 sheets, 20 x 10 each

79 (p.49)
Greg Lynn; FORM
Ark of the World, 2002
computer-generated animation on DVD; dimensions variable
Courtesy Greg Lynn; FORM

80 (p.73)
Virgilio Marchi
View of a central perimeter road, 1919
pencil on paper; 40.5 x 53
Courtesy V&A Images/V&A Museum

81 (p.48)
Virgilio Marchi
'Spatial Study', 1919
pencil on paper; 40.5 x 53
Courtesy V&A Images/V&A Museum

82 (p.52)
Marshall & Tweedy, with Oliver Bernard and Partners
Aerial perspective by Norman Howard
Design, unexecuted, for Hendon airport, London, c. 1935
photographic print of original drawing; 21.5 x 58.5

83 (p.57)
Leslie Martin
Design for a National and Government Centre, Whitehall, London, 1965
design model of wood, metal and sponge with pen added; 13 x 116.5 x 61

84 (p.48)
Raymond McGrath
Design for British Broadcasting Corporation dance and chamber music studio, Broadcasting House, Langham Place, London, 1929
gouache and silver paint on paper; 73 x 52.5

85 (p.98)
Tom Mellor
Capriccio of Notre-Dame du Haut, Ronchamp, France in ruins, 1981
pen, gouache and watercolour on paper; 44.5 x 63

86 (p.75)
Eric Mendelsohn
Design for White City, Kensington and Chelsea, London, c. 1935
crayon on paper; 29.5 x 41.5
Courtesy V&A Images/V&A Museum

87 (pp.10–11, 75)
William Cameron Menzies, director
Things to Come, 1936
film extract transferred to DVD; running time: 1 minute, 3 seconds
Produced by Alexander Korda
Set design by László Moholy-Nagy
Image supplied courtesy of Carlton International Media Limited
Photo: courtesy British Film Institute

88 (p.76)
William Noel Moffett
Design for redevelopment of Piccadilly Circus, London, 1959
pen, pencil and crayon on tracing paper; 53.5 x 78.5

89 (p.64)
MVRDV
Pig City, 2001
computer-generated image shown as digital print; dimensions variable
Courtesy MVRDV, Rotterdam
Research and design MVRDV, Rotterdam
Winy Maas, Jacob van Rijs and Nathalie de Vries with Ronald Wall, Arjan Harbers, Cord Siegel, Anton van Hoorn, Christoph Schindler, Katarzyna Glazewska and Uli Queisser
Based on initial studies by Meta Berghauser-Pont, Permeta Architecten, Amsterdam

90 (p.86)
Takehiko Nagakura
The Danteum (Guiseppe Terragni/Pietro Lingeri, 1938), 1998
computer-generated animation on DVD; running time: 5 minutes, 46 seconds
Produced by Takehiko Nagakura
Architects: Guiseppe Terragni and Pietro Lingeri, 1938
Computer Graphics: Takehiko Nagakura, Halbane Liew, Ben Black
© Massachusetts Institute of Technology, 1998

91 (p.86)
Takehiko Nagakura
Monument to the Third International (Vladimir Tatlin, 1919), 1999
computer-enhanced film on DVD; running time: 3 minutes, 12 seconds
Produced by Takehiko Nagakura
Architect: Vladimir Tatlin, 1919
Computer Graphics: Andrzej Zarzycki, Takehiko Nagakura, Dan Brick, Mark Sich
© Massachusetts Institute of Technology, 1998

92 (pp.40–41)
NASA Ames Research Center
Toroidal Colonies, c. 1970s
digital image of original painting; dimensions variable
Courtesy NASA Ames Research Center

93 (p.34)
Christopher Nicholson
Perspective by Hugh Casson
Design for the living room for the Pantheon, West Dean, West Sussex, 1938
pencil, coloured crayon and gouache on tracing paper; 19.5 x 29.5

94 (p.49)
Nils Norman
Proposed Redevelopment of the Oval, Hackney E2, London. Renamed: Let the Blood of the Private Property Developers Run Freely in the Streets of Hackney, Playscape Complex A., 2003
digital print mounted on MDF with model in mixed media; 120 x 96 x 60 (model: 120 x 96 x 77, including base) and 122 x 94 (digital drawing)
Courtesy the artist and 38 Langham Street, London

95 (p.99)
Claes Oldenburg
London Knees (Edition of 120, signed and numbered), 1966–68
latex, folder of lithographs and case; 27 x 41 x 39
Arts Council Collection, Hayward Gallery, London

96 (pp.28–29)
ORA-ÏTO
10,000Hz Legend – Air, 2001
computer-generated image shown as digital print; dimensions variable
Courtesy ORA-ÏTO
© ORA-ÏTO 2004

97 (p.84)
Andrea Palladio
Idealised reconstruction of the forum and sanctuary of Fortuna Primigenia, Palestrina (ancient Praeneste), Italy, c. 1560
pen on paper; 39 x 29

List of Works

98 (p.77)
John Buonarotti Papworth
Design, unexecuted, for Hygeia, Kentucky, USA,
1827
print (with building key) with coloured
washes added on paper; 45.5 x 65

99 (p.38)
Eric Parry
Study for Villa of the Physicists, 1985
ink on paper; 33 x 33 x 48.5
Courtesy Eric Parry Architects
© Eric Parry Architects 2004

100 (p.87)
Giovanni Pastrone, director
Cabiria, 1914
film still; dimensions variable
Produced by Giovanni Pastrone
Screenplay by Giovanni Pastrone and
Gabriel D'Annunzio
Photo: courtesy British Film Institute

101 (p.55)
Joseph Paxton
The Great Victorian Way, Sydenham, London,
1855
pen and coloured washes on paper;
104 x 70.5
Courtesy V&A Images/V&A Museum

102 (p.77)
Stephen Rowland Pierce
*Design for a post-war reconstruction of the
'Metropolis of Britain',* 1942
brown pen and wash on paper; 52 x 36.5

103 (p.55)
Giovanni Battista Piranesi
Imaginary Prison, plate XIV, 2nd edition, 1761
print; 41 x 53
Courtesy RIBA Library

104 (p.89)
Arthur Beresford Pite
*Competition design for a 'West-End Club House',
for the Soane Medallion Prize,* 1882
pen on paper; 102.5 x 62.5

105
Cedric Price
Sketch for Fun Palace for Joan Littlewood, 1974
ink sketch, with pencil and watercolour on
watercolour paper; 25 x 17.5
Private Collection
Image on p.102:
Interior View for the Fun Palace, 1951–65
pen with white and black ink and graphite
over a gelatin silver print of the model; 12.5
x 24.9; DR1995:0188:518
© Cedric Price Archive, Collection
Canadian Centre for Architecture,
Montreal 2004

106 (p.71)
Gaston Quiribet, director
The Fugitive Futurist: A Q-riosity by 'Q', 1924
film extract transferred to DVD; running
time: 3 minutes
Produced by Cecil M. Hepworth
Courtesy Cecil M. Hepworth
© C.M. Hepworth 2004
Photo: courtesy British Film Institute

107 (p.64)
Thomas Rickman and Richard Charles
Hussey
*Competition design for the Fitzwilliam Museum,
Cambridge,* 1834
pencil and watercolour on paper; 82 x 60

108 (pp.90–91)
John Pollard Seddon and Edward Beckitt
Lamb
*Design for the Imperial Monumental Halls and
Tower, Westminster, London,* 1904
watercolour on board; 65 x 91.5

109 (p.65)
R. Seifert and Partners
Perspective by A.F. Gill
*Design for an office building, Melbourne,
Australia,* c. 1970
pen, gouache and coloured crayon on card;
66 x 100

110 (p.47)
Geoff Shearcroft/AOC
Grow Your Own, 2001
computer-generated image shown
as digital print; dimensions variable
Courtesy Geoff Shearcroft

111 (p.37)
John Smythson, attributed
Design for a pavilion in a formal landscape,
c. 1620
pen, pencil and brown and green washes
on paper; 43 x 28

112 (p.36)
Robert Smythson
Design for a house in the form of a Greek cross,
c. 1580s
pen and wash on paper; 13.4 x 13.5

113 (p.98)
John Soane
Copy by Charles James Richardson, after
original perspective by J.M. Gandy
*'Architectural visions of early fancy in the gay
morning of youth and dreams in the evening of
life',* c. 1825
pen, pencil and brown wash on paper;
34.5 x 56
Courtesy V&A Images/V&A Museum

114 (p.38)
Softroom
Floating Retreat, 1997
computer-generated animation on DVD
Courtesy Softroom
© Softroom 2004

115
Softroom
Maison Canif, 1997
computer-generated animation on DVD
Courtesy Softroom
© Softoom 2004

116
Softroom
Supersonic Private Jet, 1998
computer-generated animation on DVD
Courtesy Softroom
© Softroom 2004

117
Softroom
Time Future Den, 1998
computer-generated animation on DVD
Courtesy Softroom
© Softroom 2004

118
Softroom
Treehouse, 1998
computer-generated animation on DVD
Courtesy Softroom
© Softoom 2004

119 (p.33)
Softroom
Lollyworld, 1999
computer-enhanced pop music video
shown on DVD
Courtesy Softroom
Setting for the video to single 'Big Boys
Don't Cry' by Lolly. Directed by Softroom
© 1999 Polydor Records

120 (p.65)
Paolo Soleri
Design for an arcology, 1977
black marker pen on paper; 28 x 21

121 (p.58)
Superstudio
The Continuous Monument – New New York,
1969
lithograph, 100 x 70
Archivio Superstudio, Firenze
© Archivio Superstudio 2004

122
Superstudio
New New York redevelopment, 1969
View of Manhattan looking south, 1969
New York dalla terrazza, 1969
ink on tracing paper; three sheets, 29 x 37
each, on board, 100 x 70
Collection Adolfo Natalini, Firenze
© Adolfo Natalini 2004

123
Rodney Thomas
Design for Sky City and Trees, 1938
collage with gouache and watercolour on
paper; 50.5 x 65.5

124 (p.79)
Rodney Thomas
Design for Sky City, c. 1965
pen and coloured crayons on tracing paper;
45 x 65

125 (p.66)
Philip Armstrong Tilden
*Design for a tower for Selfridges department store,
Oxford Street, London*, 1918
pen on paper; 103 x 68

126 (p.33)
Ushida Findlay
Design for Grafton New Hall, 2001
computer-generated animation on DVD;
running time: 15 minutes
Courtesy Ushida Findlay (UK) Ltd
Developer: Ferrario, Burns, Hood Ltd
© Ferrario, Burns, Hood Ltd 2004

127
Ushida Findlay
Model by Kathryn Findlay
*Grafton New Hall; working model with ping-
pong balls*, 2001
mixed media; 7 x 34 x 25.5
Courtesy Ushida Findlay (UK) Ltd
© Ushida Findlay (UK) Ltd 2004

128 (p.66)
King Vidor, director
The Fountainhead, 1949
film still; dimensions variable
Produced by Warner Brothers
Courtesy of Turner Entertainment Co.
THE FOUNTAINHEAD
© 1949 Turner Entertainment Co.
A Warner Bros. Entertainment Company.
All Rights Reserved
Photo: courtesy British Film Institute

129 (p.39)
Charles Francis Annesley Voysey
*Design for a wallpaper or textile, called 'The
Dream'*, 1889
pen and coloured washes on paper; 43 x 30

130 (p.88)
William Walcot
*Reconstruction of the Temple of Diana, Ephesus,
Turkey*, 1923
watercolour and gouache on paper;
83 x 119

131 (pp.60–61)
Alfred Waterhouse
*Competition design for the Royal Courts
of Justice, Strand, London*, 1866
pen with brown and grey washes on paper;
84.5 x 113.6

132 (pp.80–81)
Paul Wegener and Carl Boese, directors
The Golem, 1920
film still; dimensions variable
Produced by Paul Davidson
Production design by Hans Poelzig
Rights: Friedrich-Wilhelm-Murnau-
Stiftung
Distributor: Transit Film GmbH
Photo: courtesy British Film Institute

133 (p.67)
Wim Wenders, director
Until the End of the World, 1991
film still; dimensions variable
Produced by Jonathan Taplin and
Anatole Dauman
'Endless Tower' designed by Jean Nouvel
© Reverse Angle Library 2004

134 (p.36)
Clough Williams-Ellis
Perspective by H.F. Waring
*Capriccio for rebuilding Plas Brondanw,
Merioneth, Wales*, 1913
pencil, pen and watercolour on paper;
44 x 61.5

135 (p.79)
Clough Williams-Ellis
*Preliminary plan and (insert) elevation for
Melcomb Satellite Town*, 1945
pencil and coloured crayons on tracing
paper; 58 x 75

List of Figures

All measurements are in cm and are height x width x depth. Page references are to illustrations in this book.